MANDALA FUN
Adult Coloring Book Volume 3

Illustrated by Cheryl Colors
#cherylcolors

www.adultcoloringworldwide.com
www.globaldoodlegems.wordpress.com

Copyright © 2016 Cheryl Colors
All rights reserved.
Published by Global Doodle Gems and Adult Coloring Worldwide.
ISBN-13: 978-8793449121 / ISBN-10: 8793449127

Front cover by Kristin Eunice.

Formatting and editing by #anniecolors

FIND US:

#cherylcolors: www.facebook.com/cherylcolors

#anniecolors: www.facebook.com/anniecolorsww

#angelacolorz: www.facebook.com/angelacolorz

LET'S GET COLORING!

• USE THIS PAGE TO TEST YOUR COLORS •

Tip: Placing an extra sheet of paper underneath your coloring pages can help to prevent bleed-through when using markers.

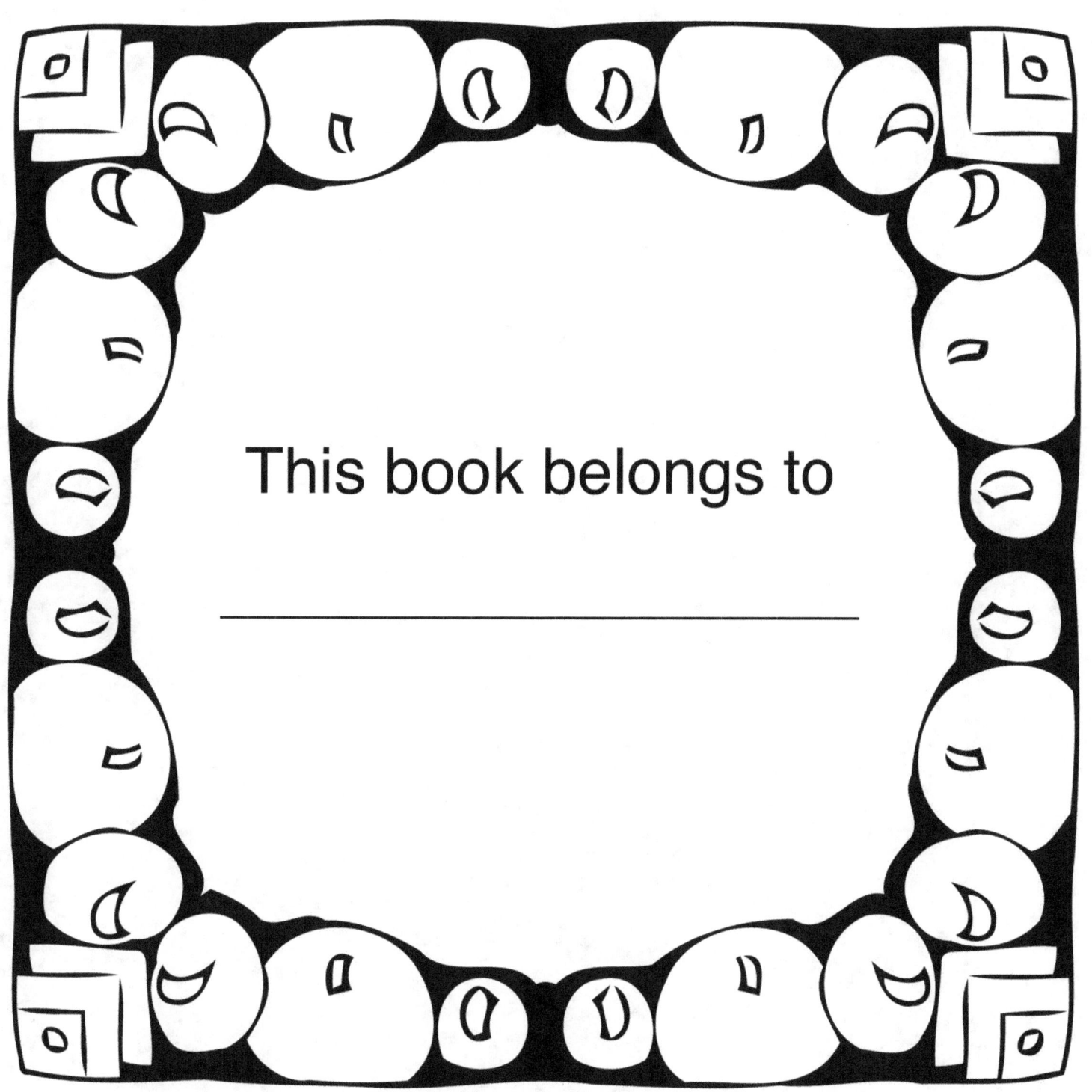

This book belongs to

_____

Illustrated by #cherylcolors
www.facebook.com/cherylcolors

Colored by: _____

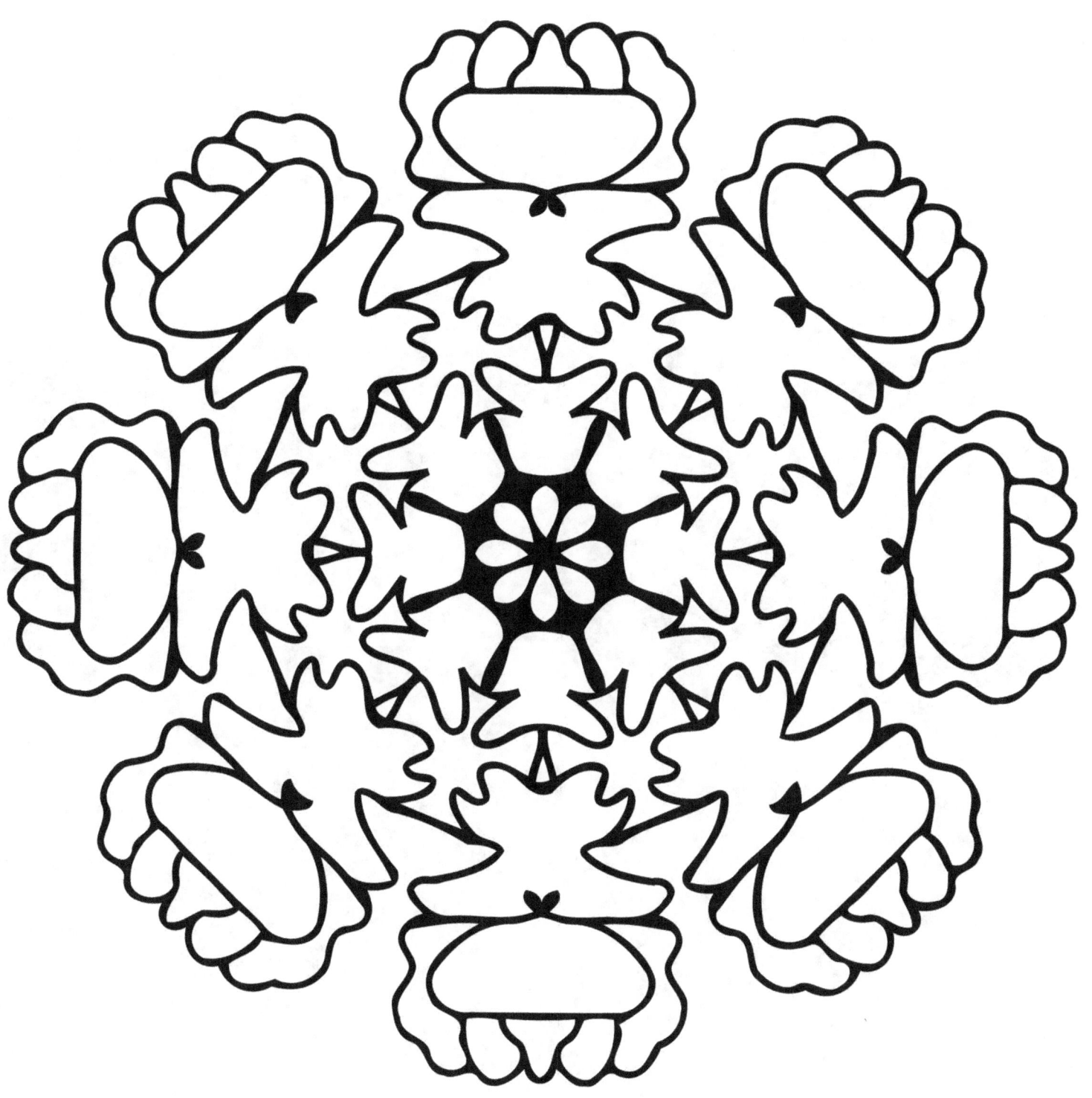

Illustrated by #cherylcolors
www.facebook.com/cherylcolors

Colored by: _____

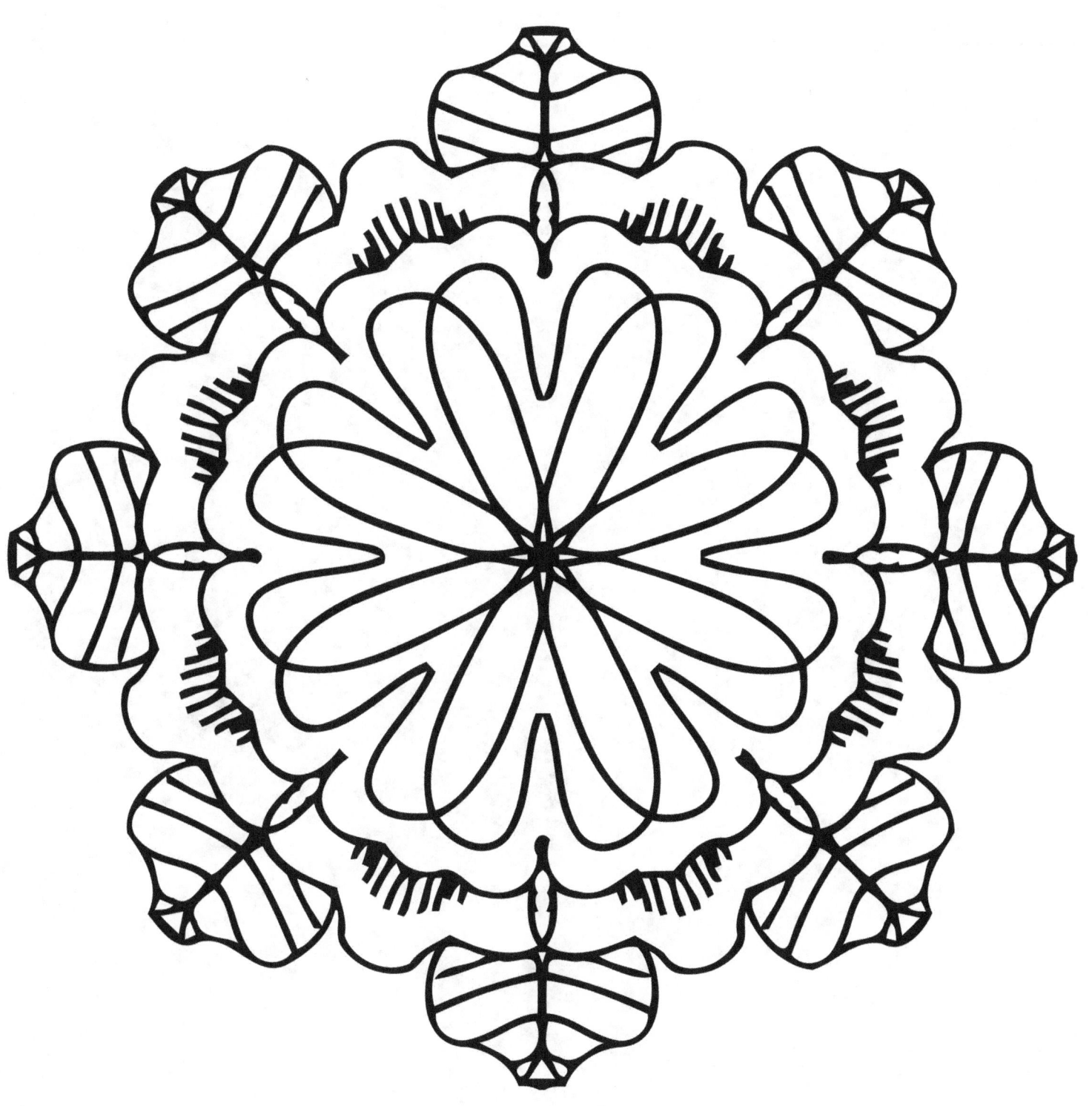

Illustrated by #cherylcolors
www.facebook.com/cherylcolors

Colored by: _____

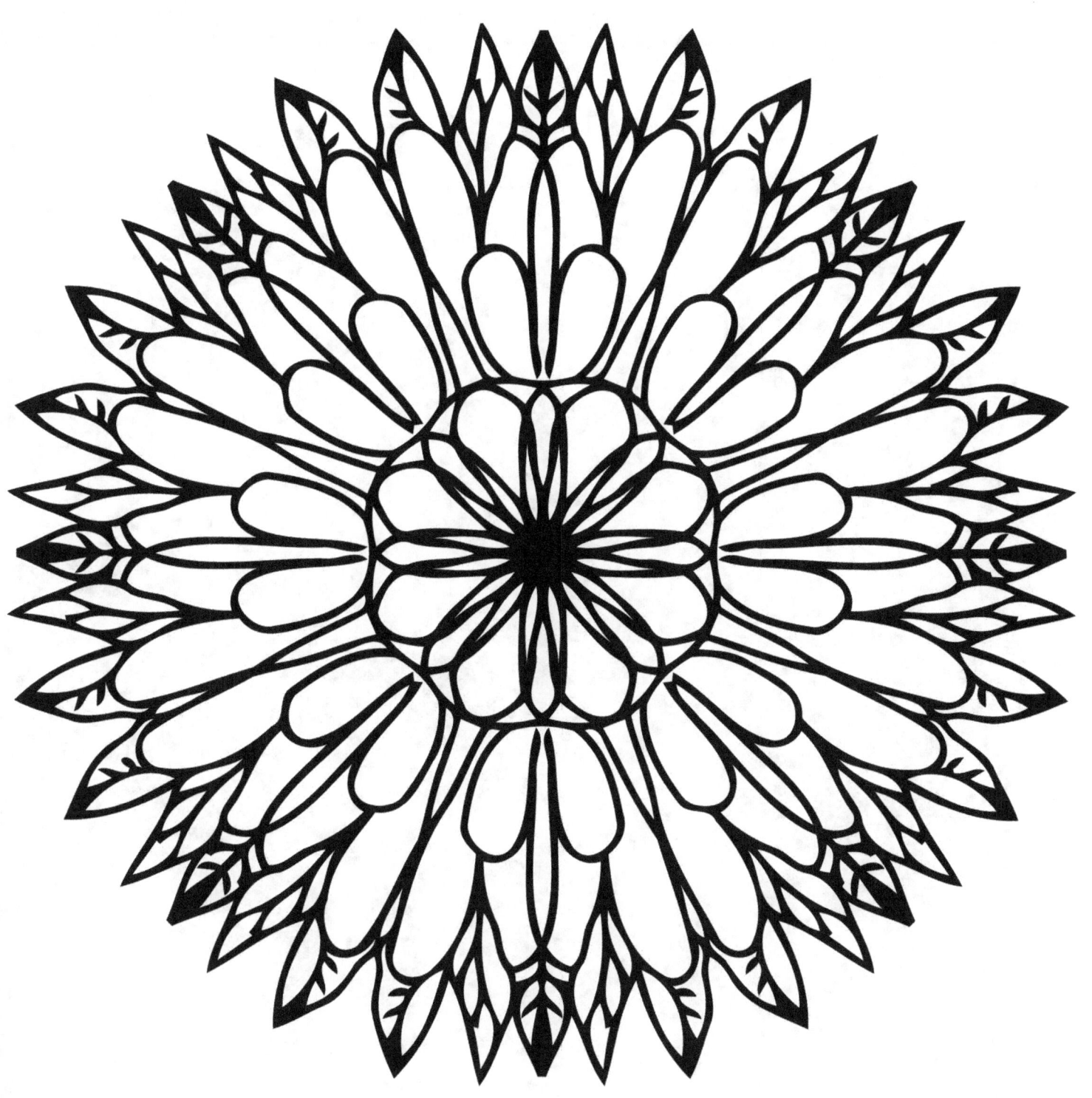

Illustrated by #cherylcolors
www.facebook.com/cherylcolors

Colored by: _____

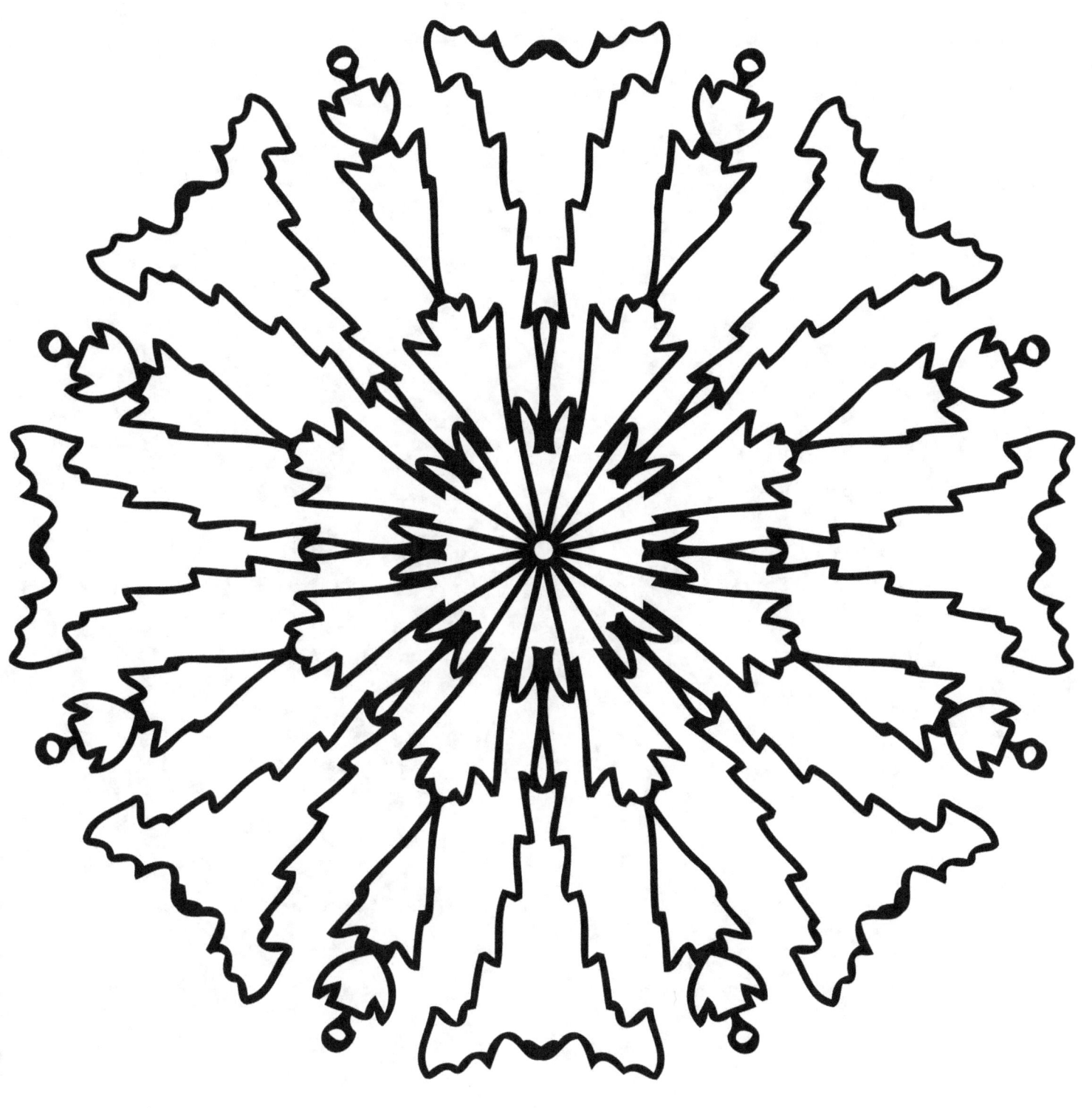

Illustrated by #cherylcolors
www.facebook.com/cherylcolors

Colored by: _____

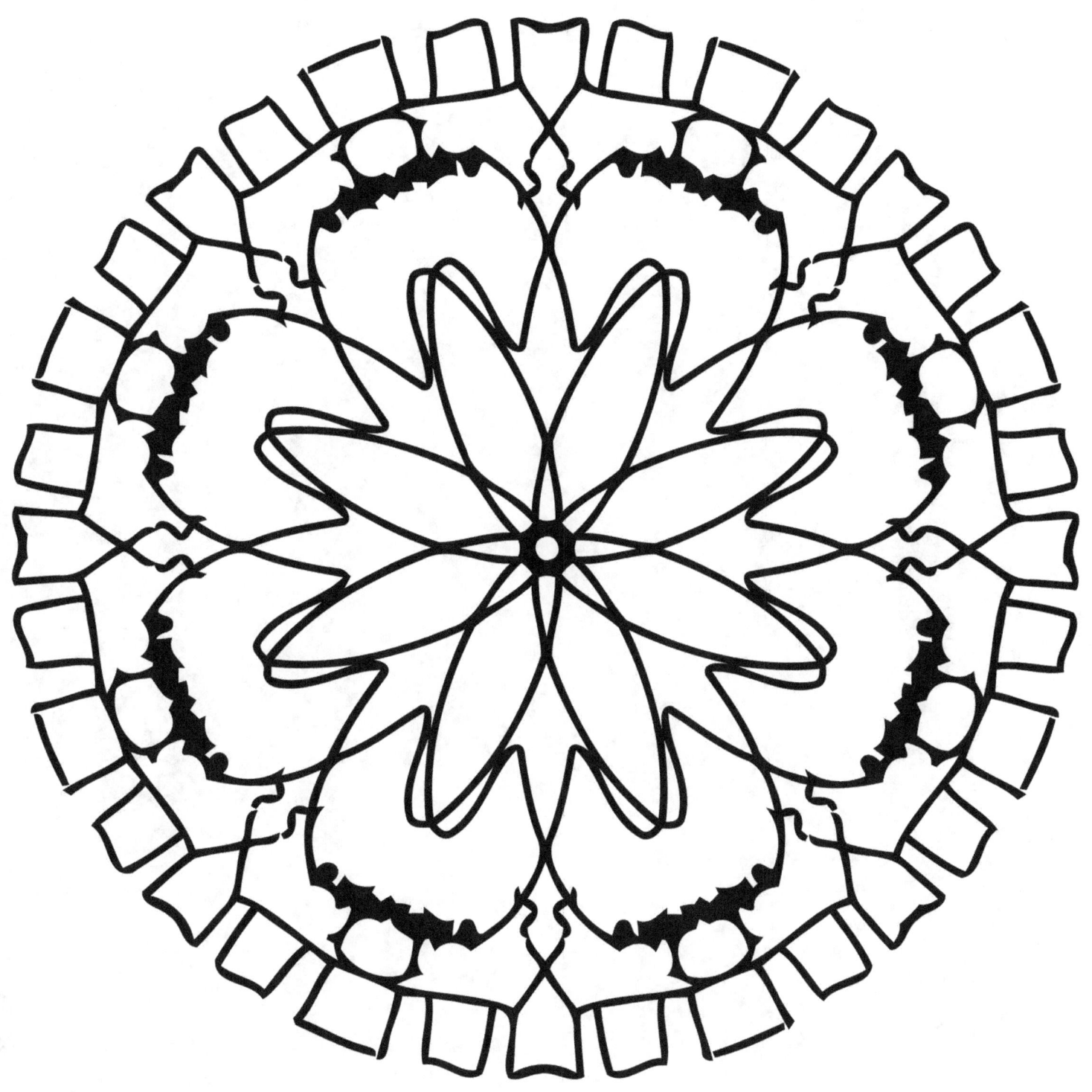

Illustrated by #cherylcolors
www.facebook.com/cherylcolors

Colored by: _____

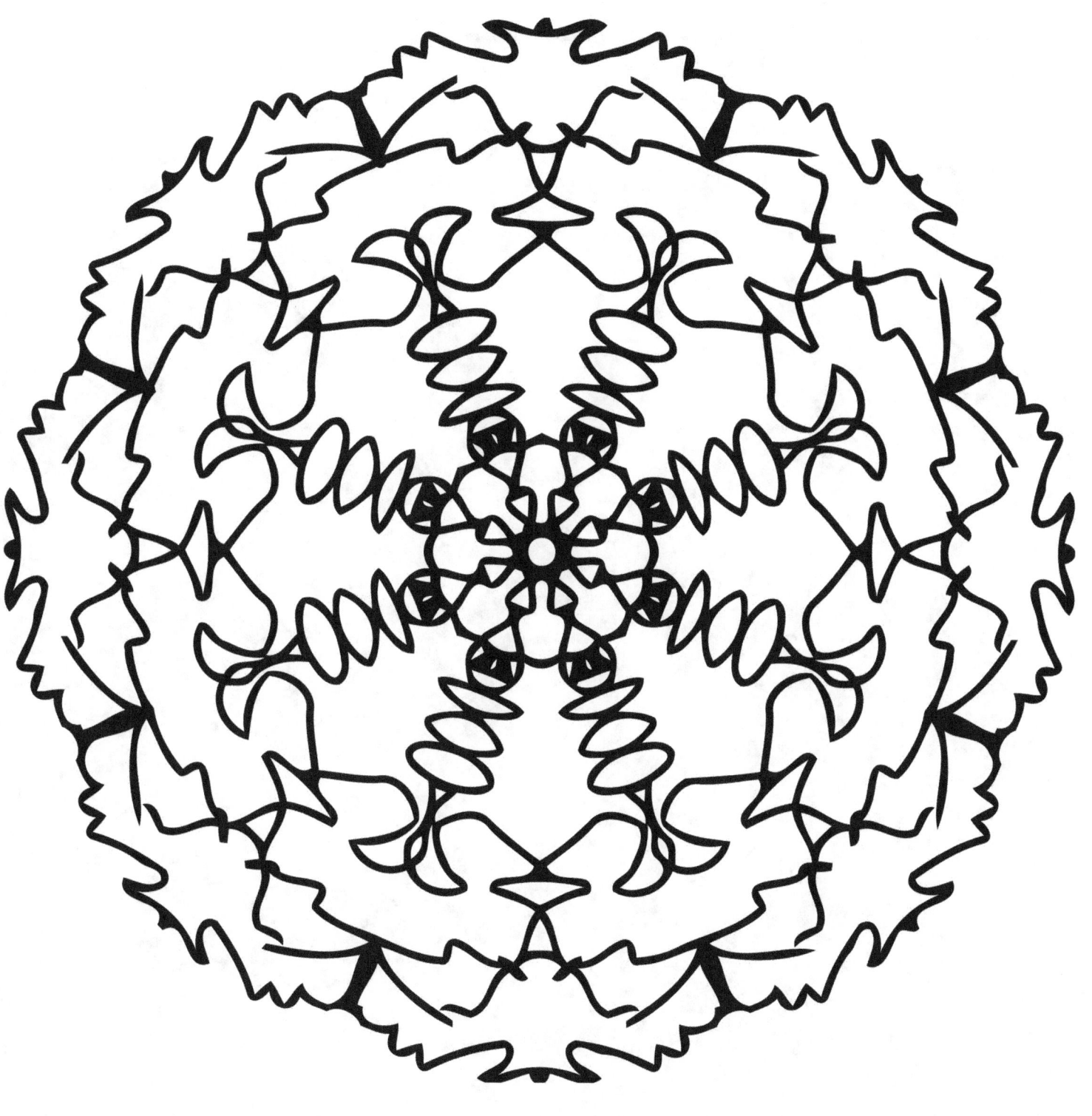

Illustrated by #cherylcolors
www.facebook.com/cherylcolors

Colored by: _____

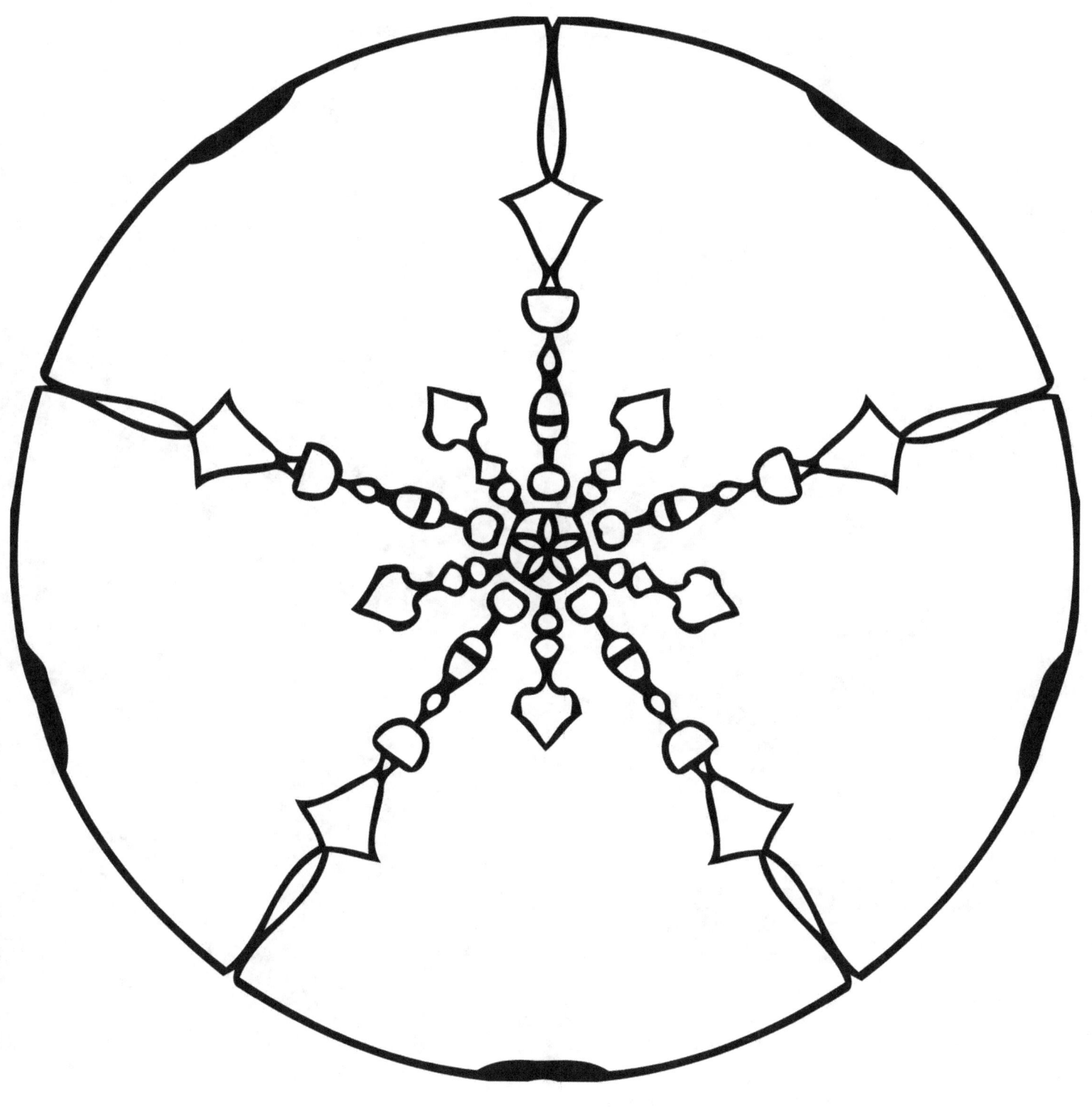

Illustrated by #cherylcolors
www.facebook.com/cherylcolors

Colored by: _____

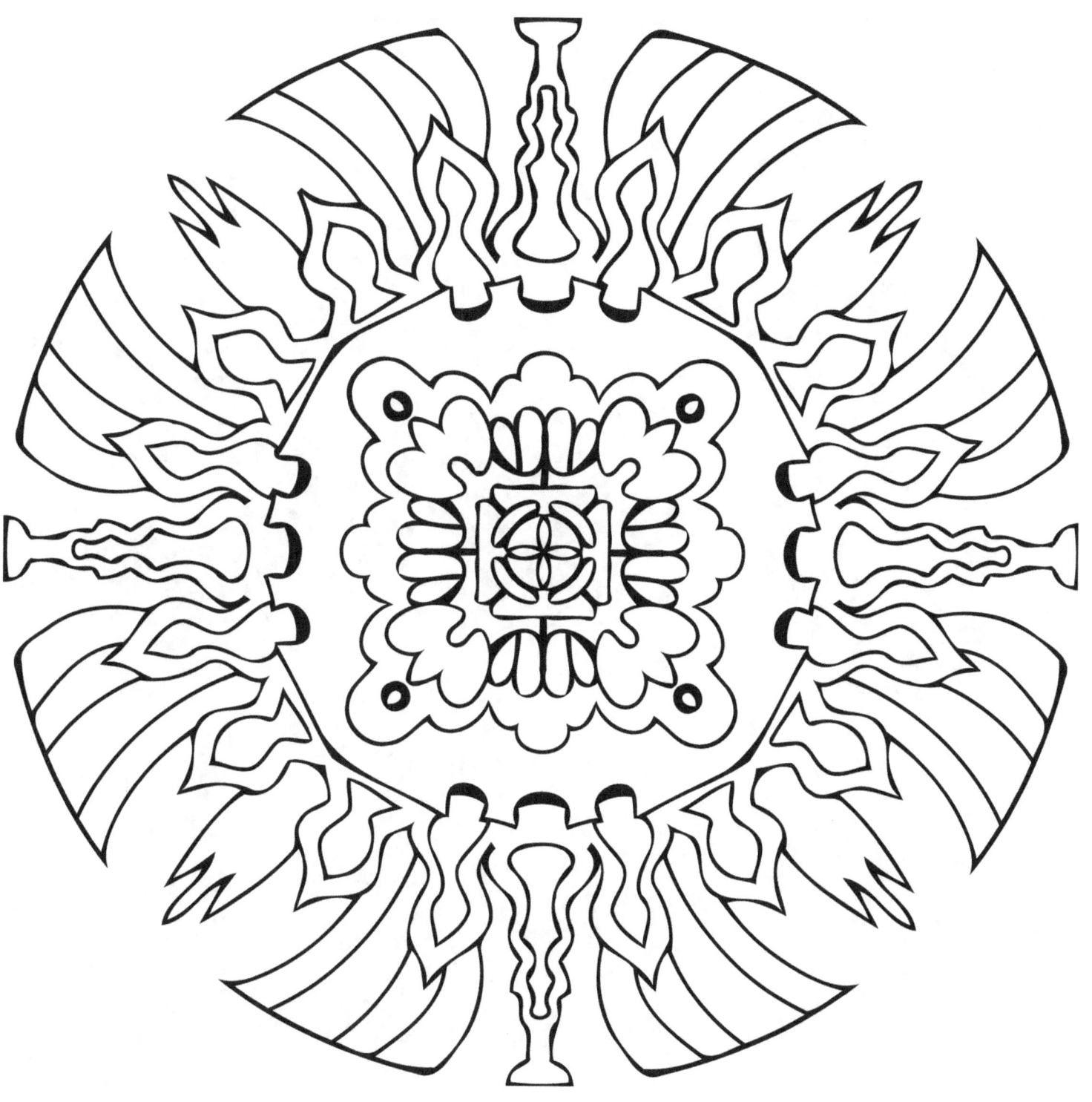

Illustrated by #cherylcolors
www.facebook.com/cherylcolors

Colored by: _____

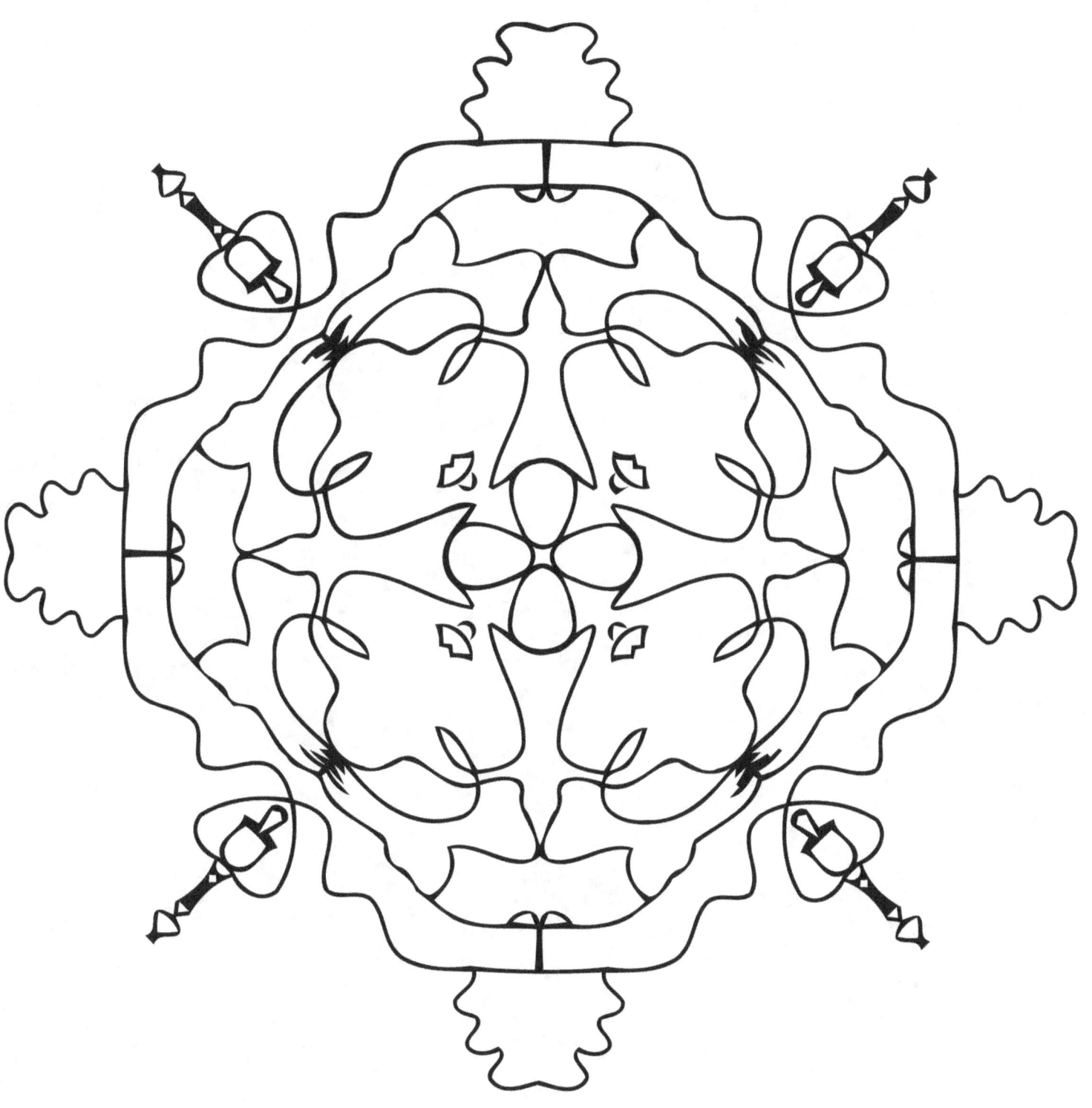

Illustrated by #cherylcolors
www.facebook.com/cherylcolors

Colored by: _____

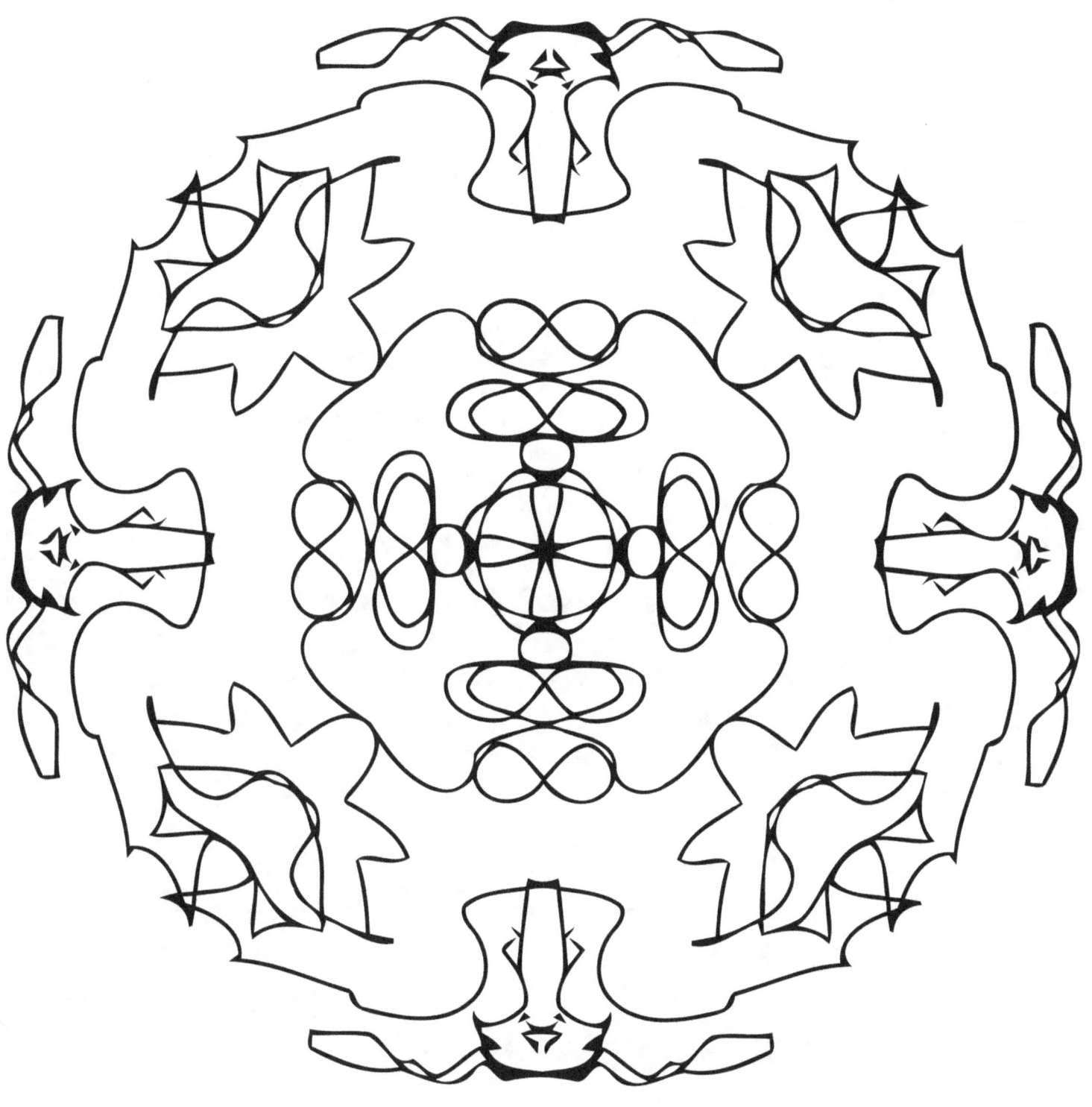

Illustrated by #cherylcolors
www.facebook.com/cherylcolors

Colored by: _____

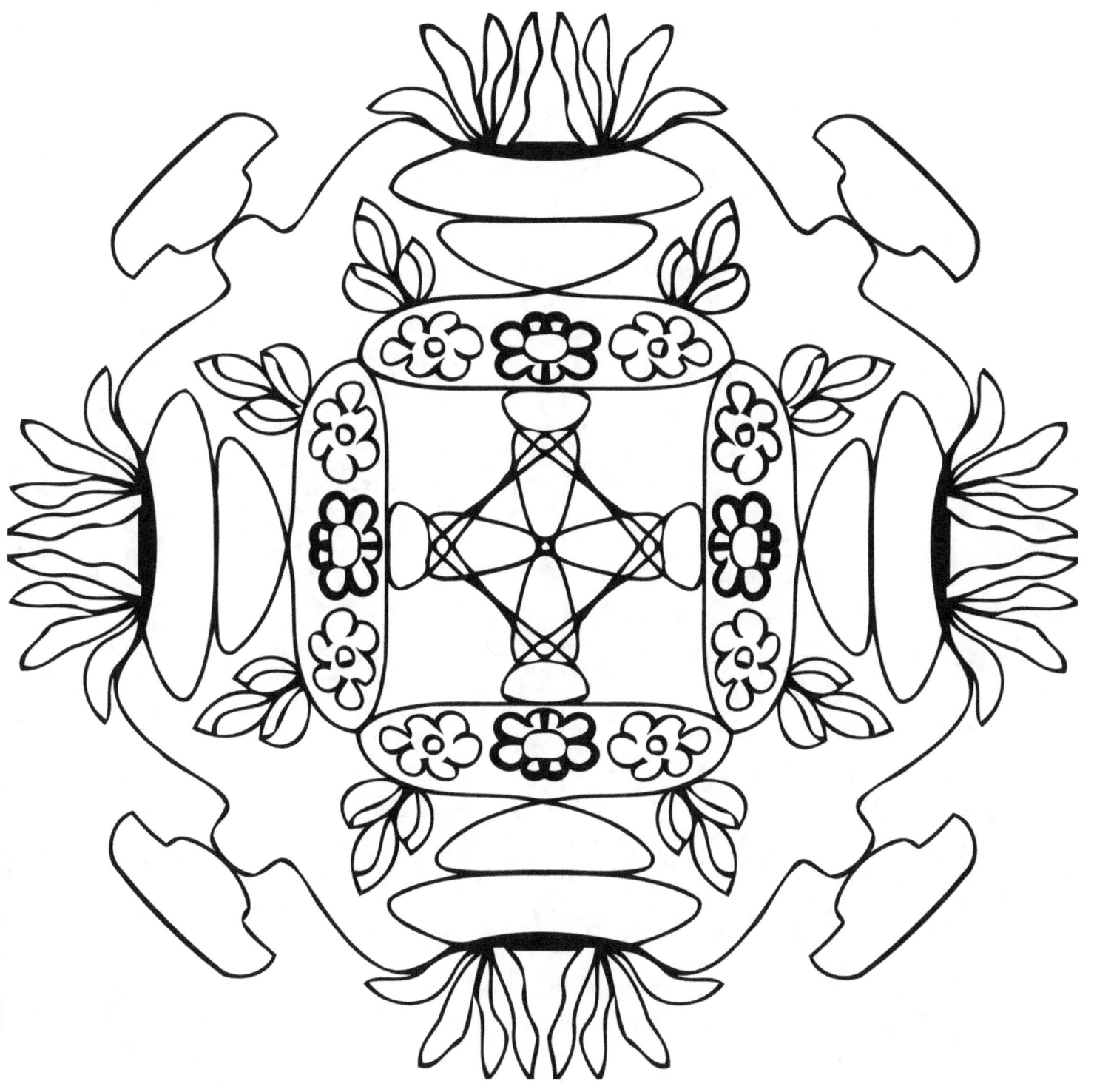

Illustrated by #cherylcolors
www.facebook.com/cherylcolors

Colored by: _____

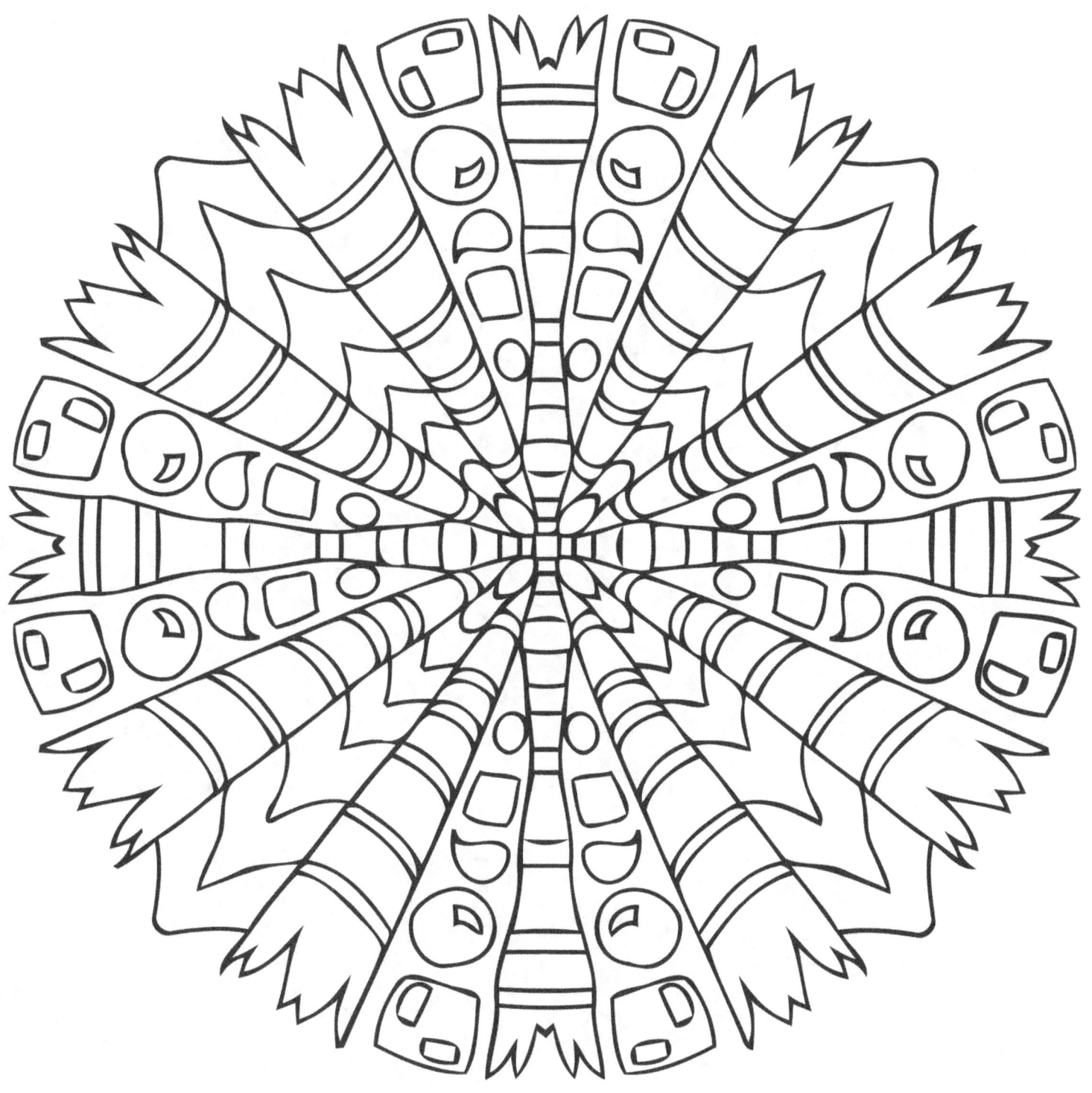

Illustrated by #cherylcolors
www.facebook.com/cherylcolors

Colored by: _____

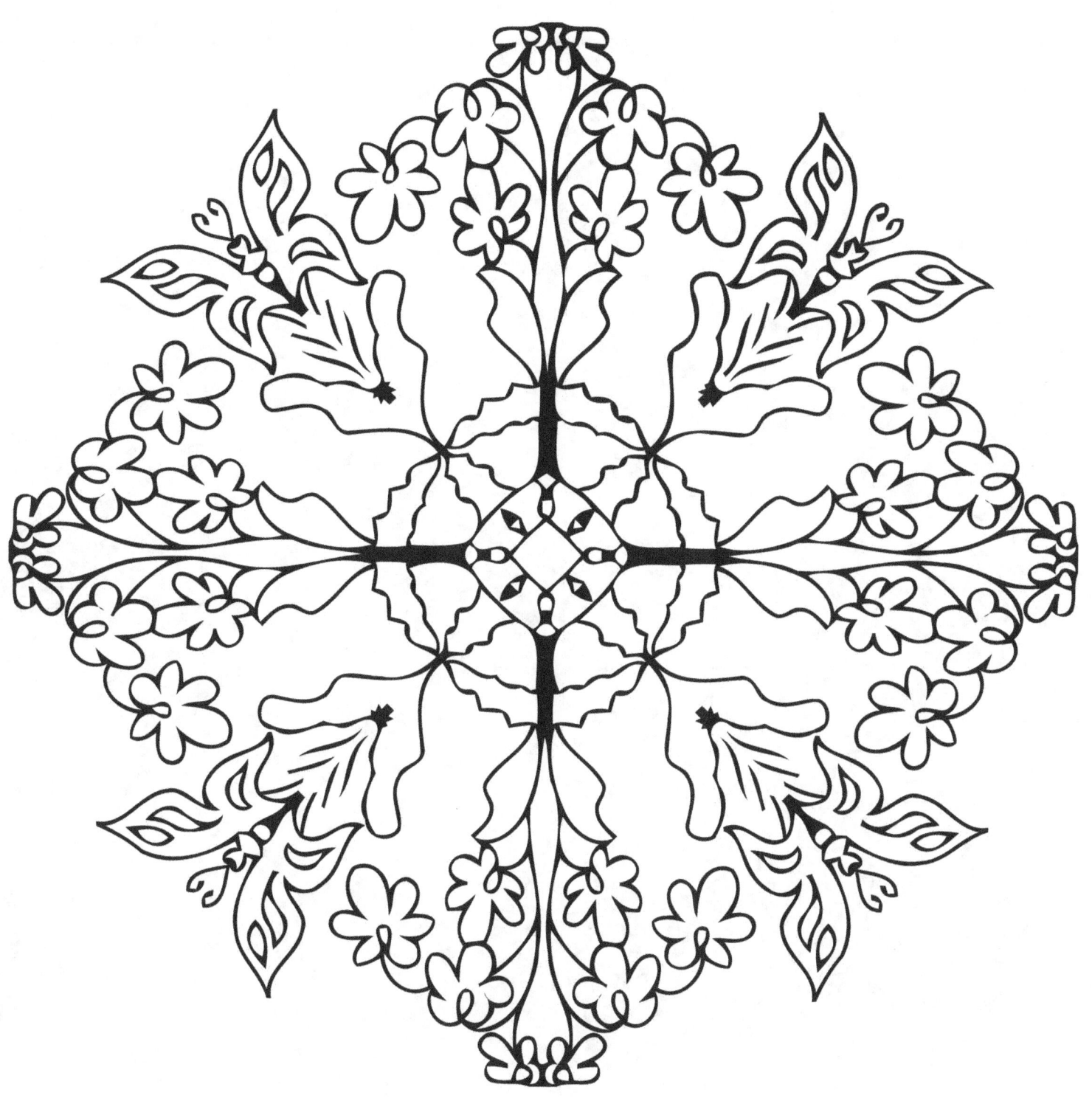

Illustrated by #cherylcolors
www.facebook.com/cherylcolors

Colored by: _____

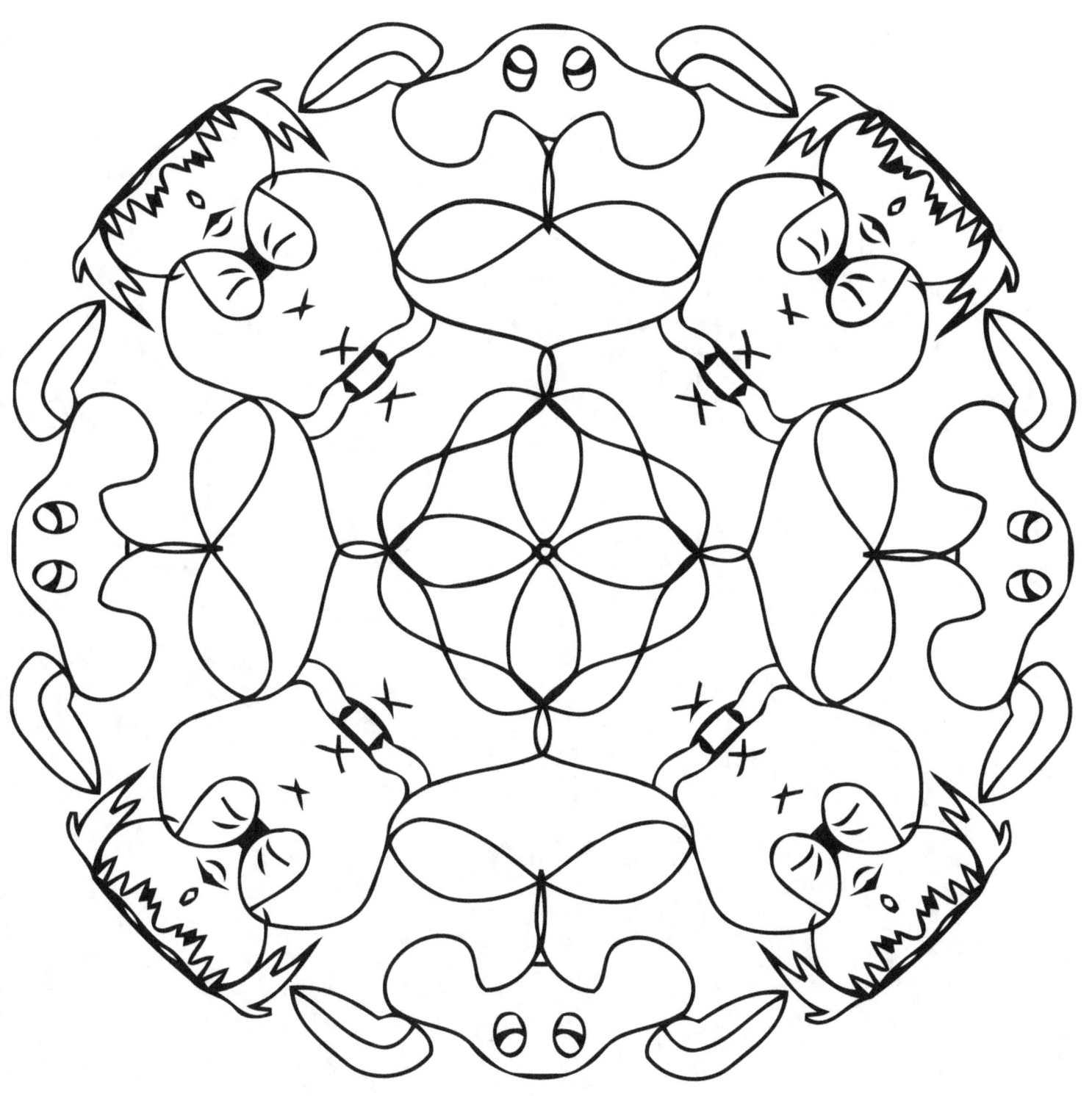

Illustrated by #cherylcolors
www.facebook.com/cherylcolors

Colored by: _____

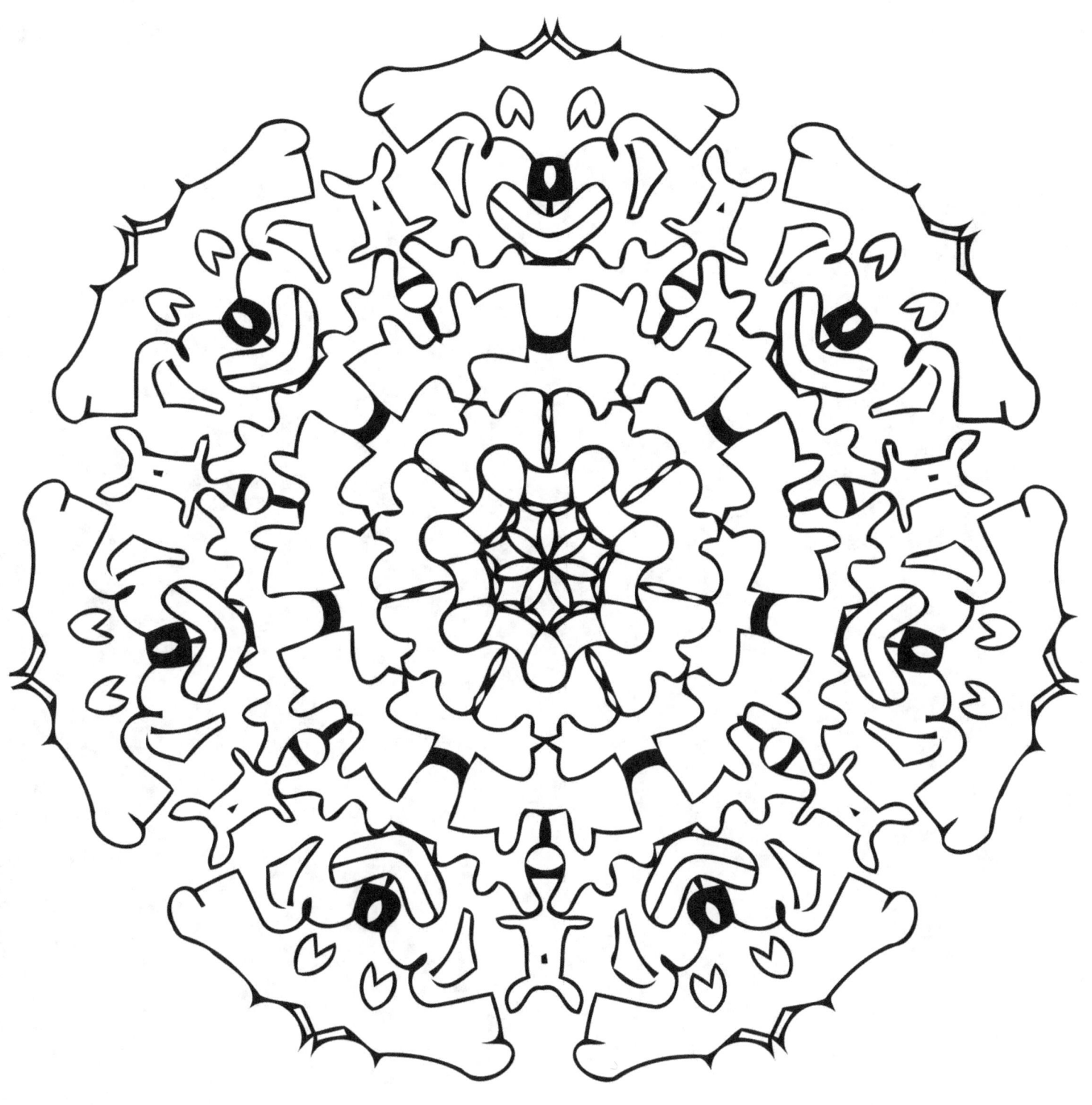

Illustrated by #cherylcolors
www.facebook.com/cherylcolors

Colored by: _____

Illustrated by #cherylcolors
www.facebook.com/cherylcolors

Colored by: _____

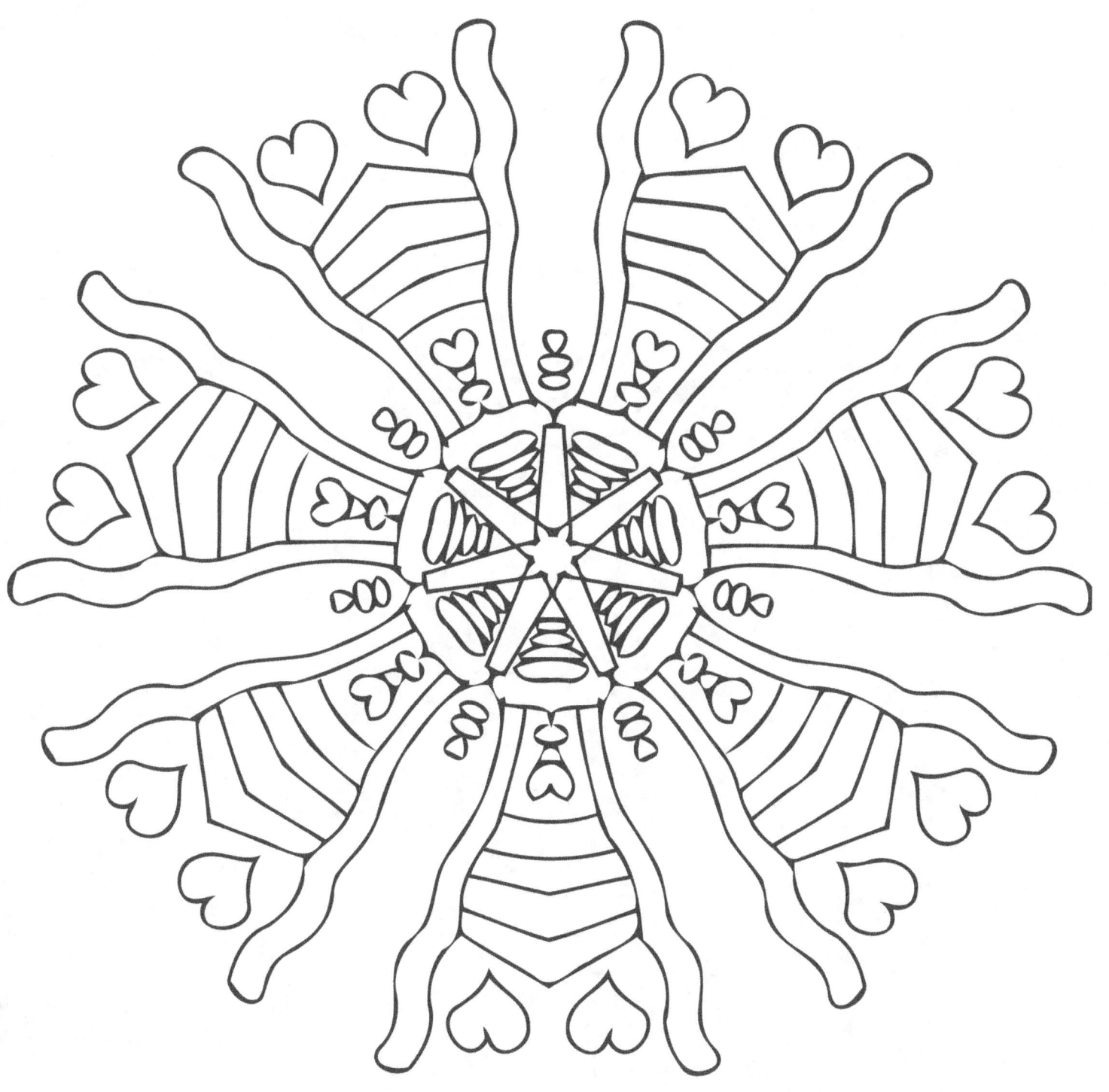

Illustrated by #cherylcolors
www.facebook.com/cherylcolors

Colored by: _____

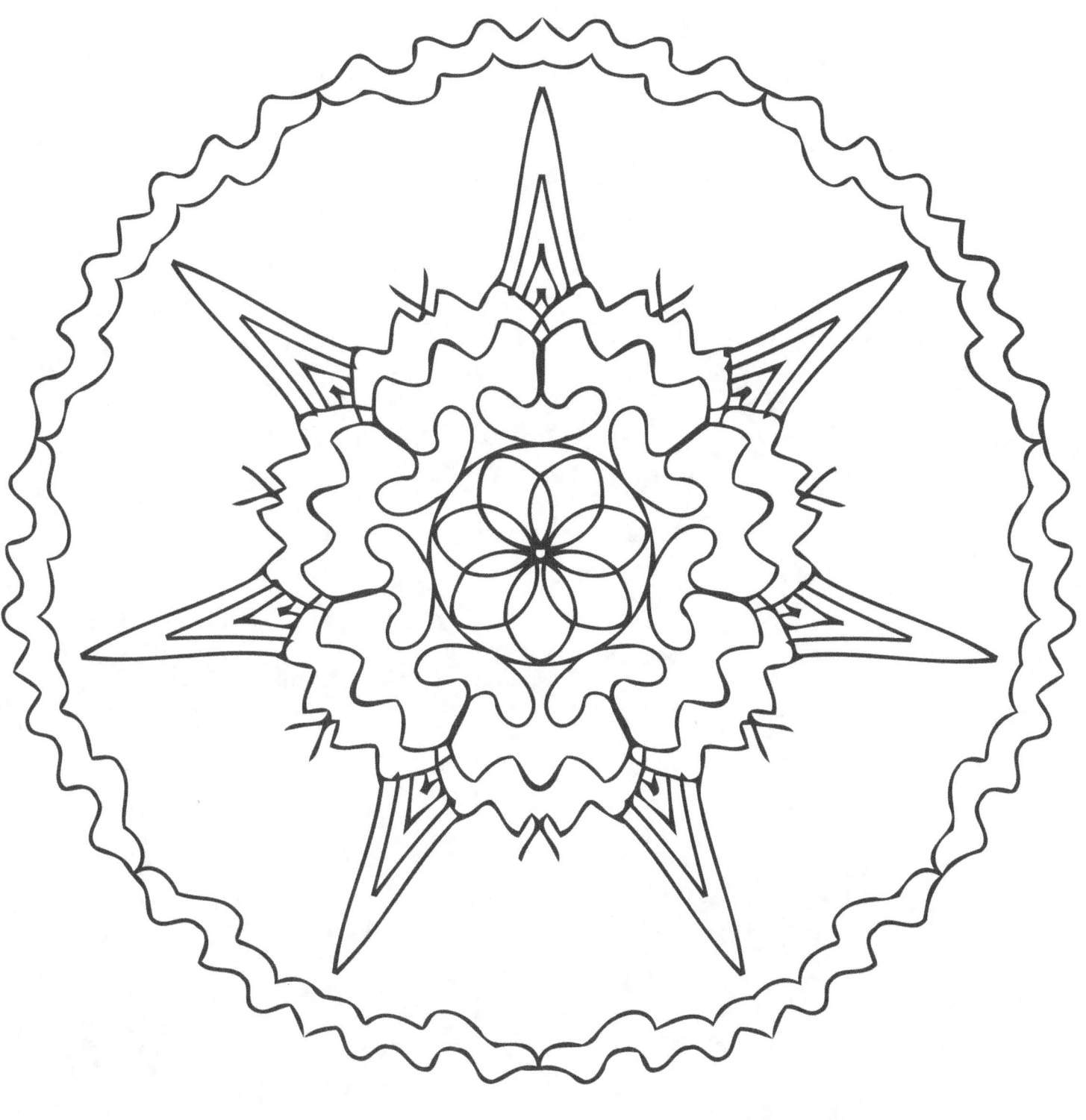

Illustrated by #cherylcolors
www.facebook.com/cherylcolors

Colored by: _____

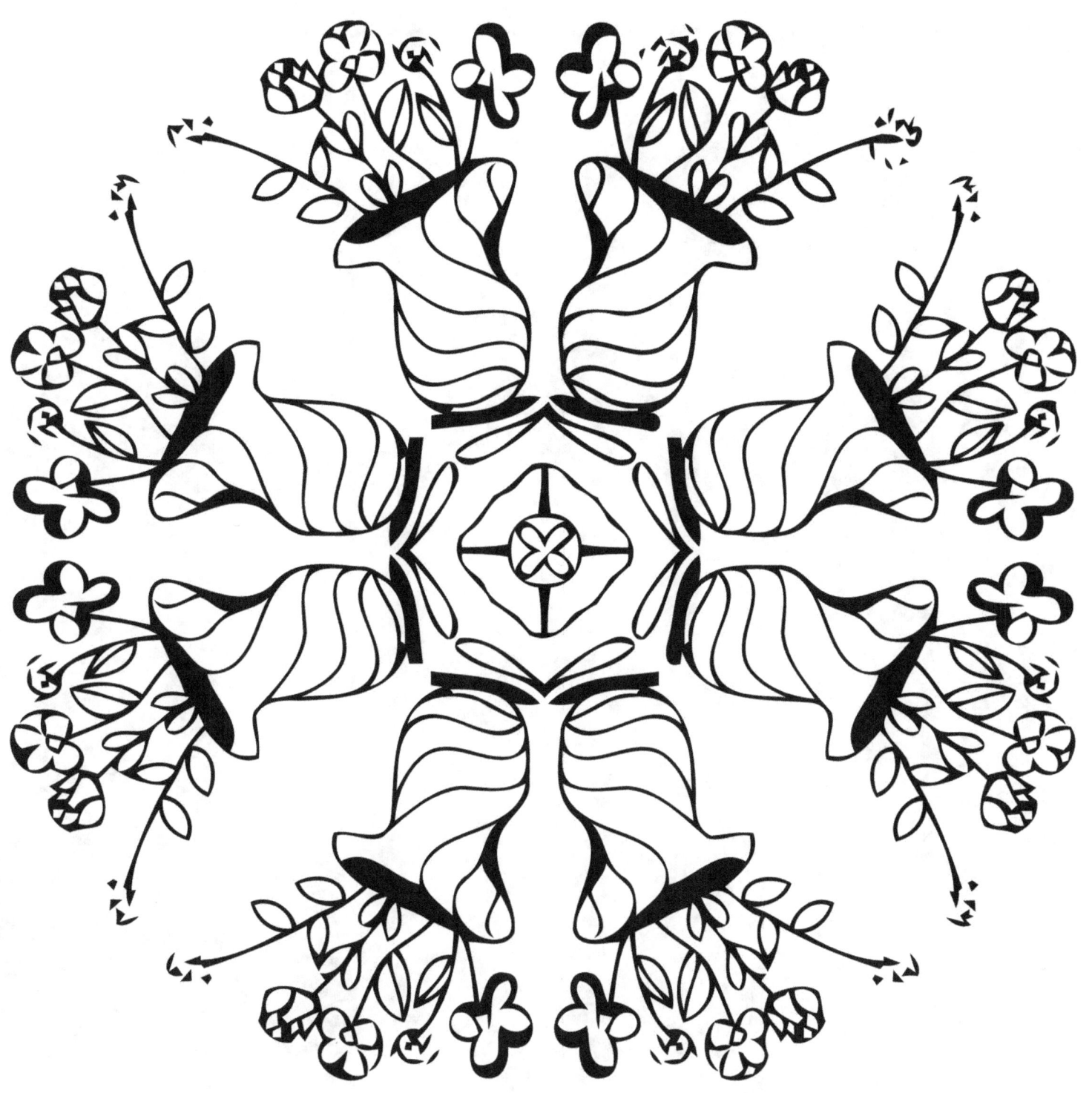

Illustrated by #cherylcolors
www.facebook.com/cherylcolors

Colored by: _____

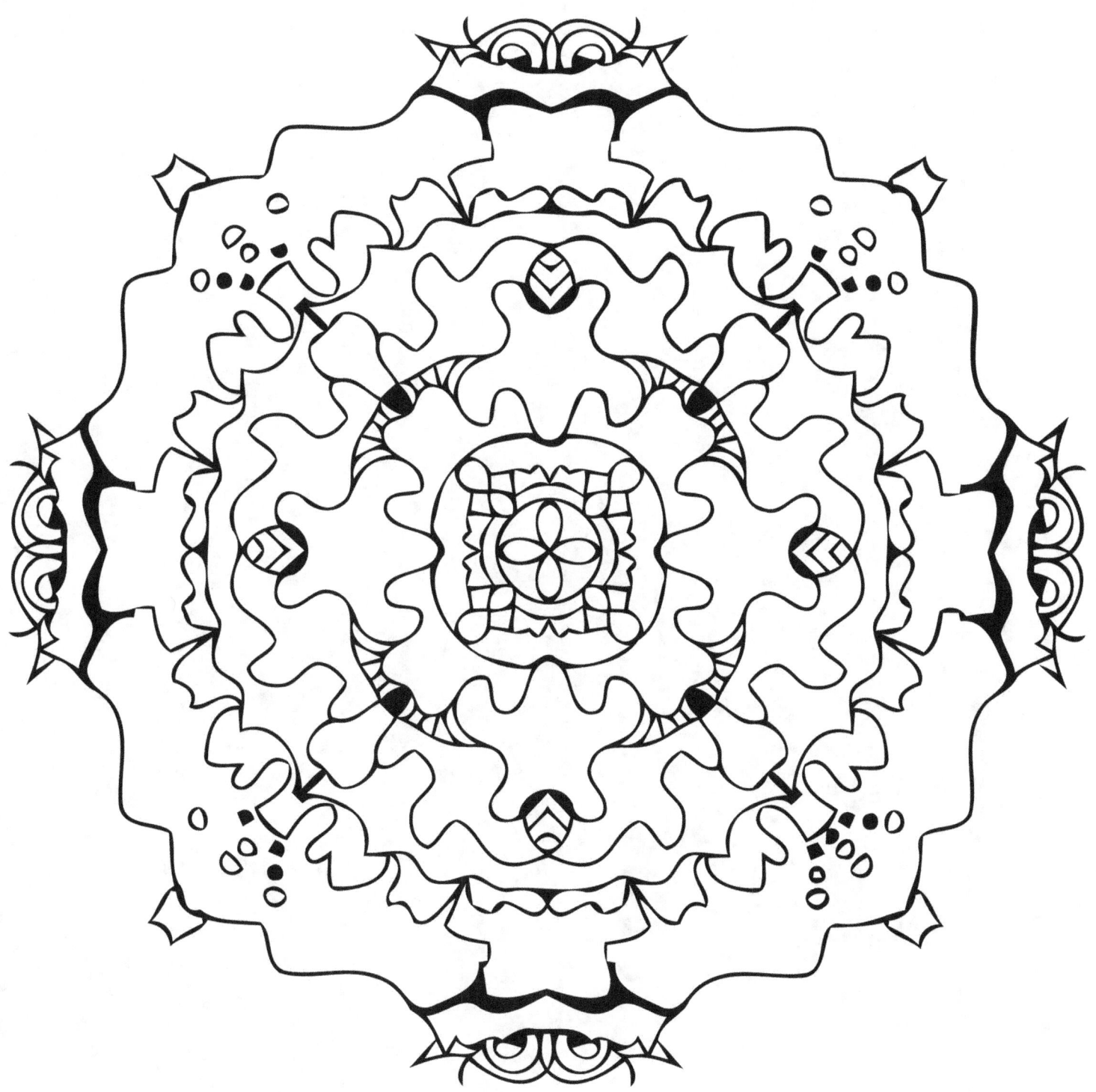

Illustrated by #cherylcolors
www.facebook.com/cherylcolors

Colored by: _____

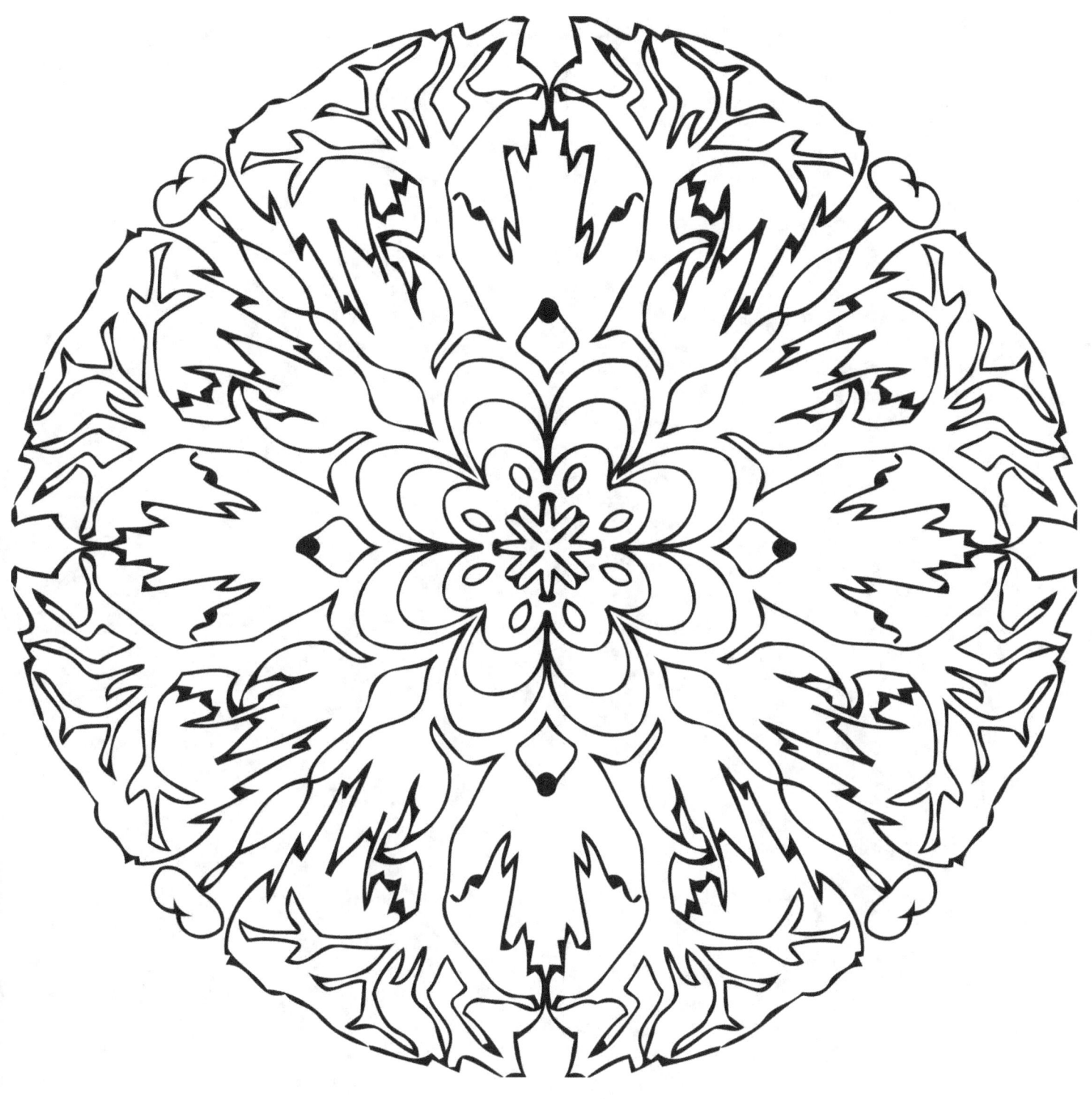

Illustrated by #cherylcolors
www.facebook.com/cherylcolors

Colored by: _____

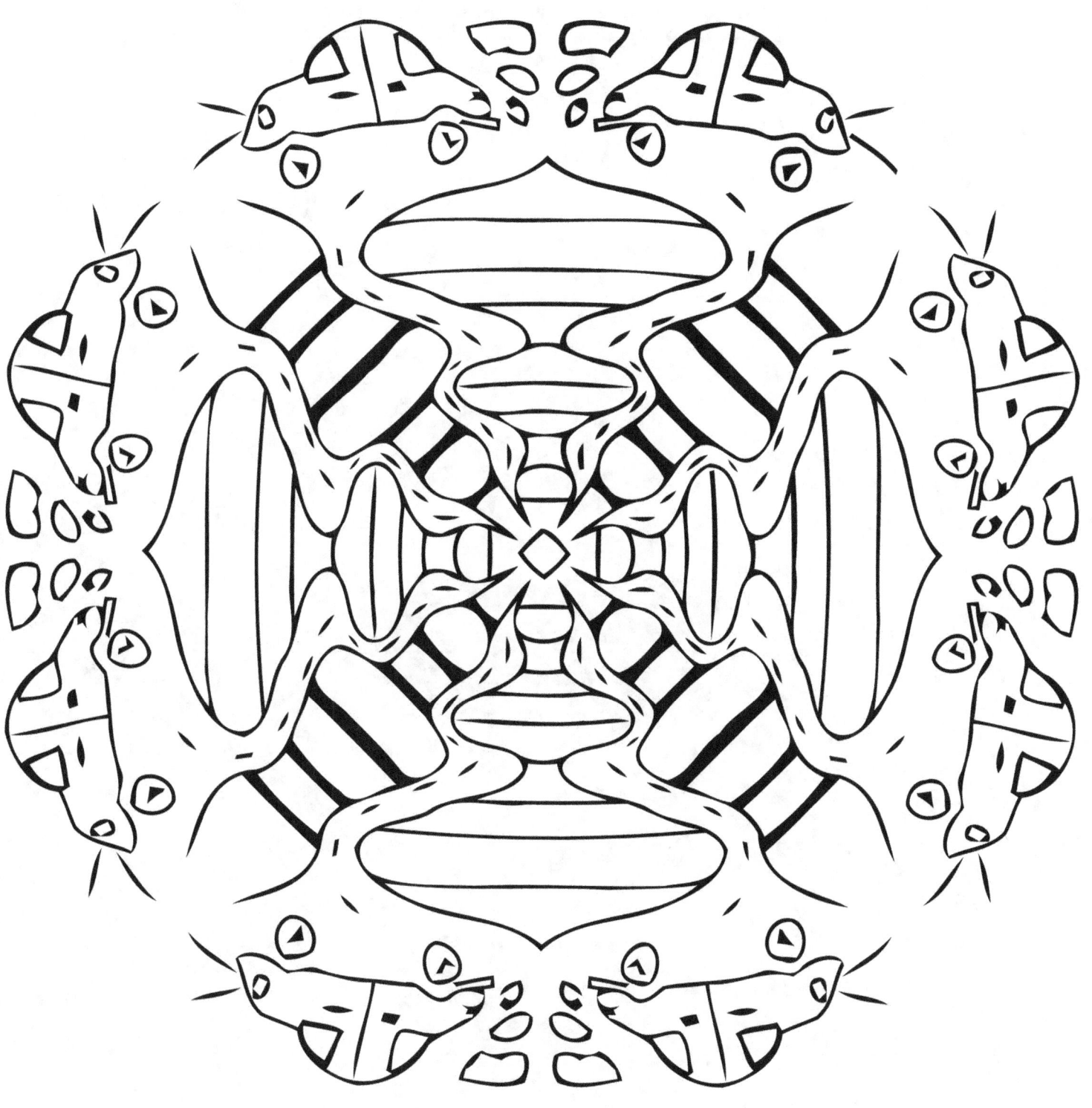

Illustrated by #cherylcolors
www.facebook.com/cherylcolors

Colored by: _____

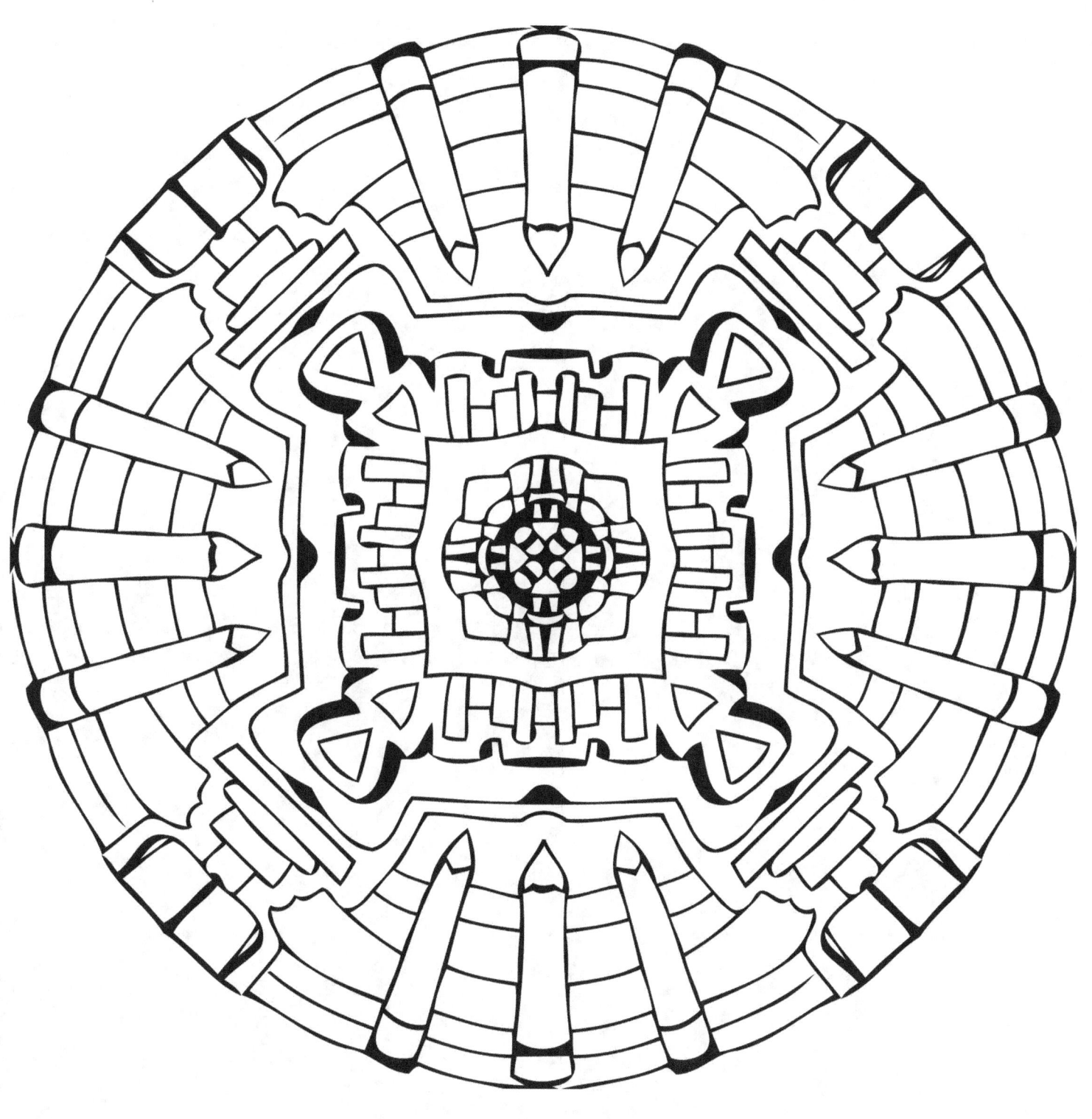

Illustrated by #cherylcolors
www.facebook.com/cherylcolors

Colored by: _____

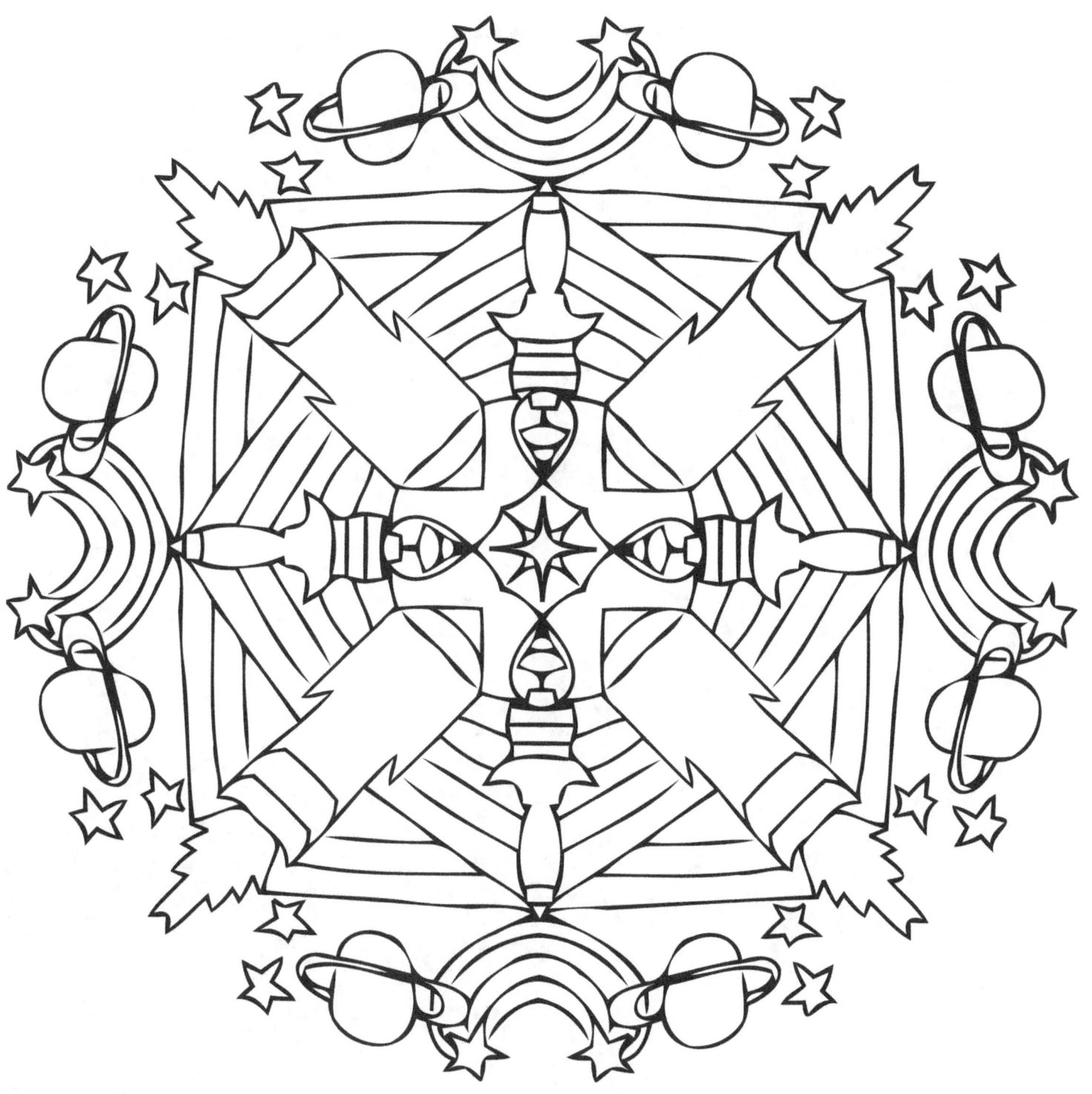

Illustrated by #cherylcolors
www.facebook.com/cherylcolors   Colored by: _____

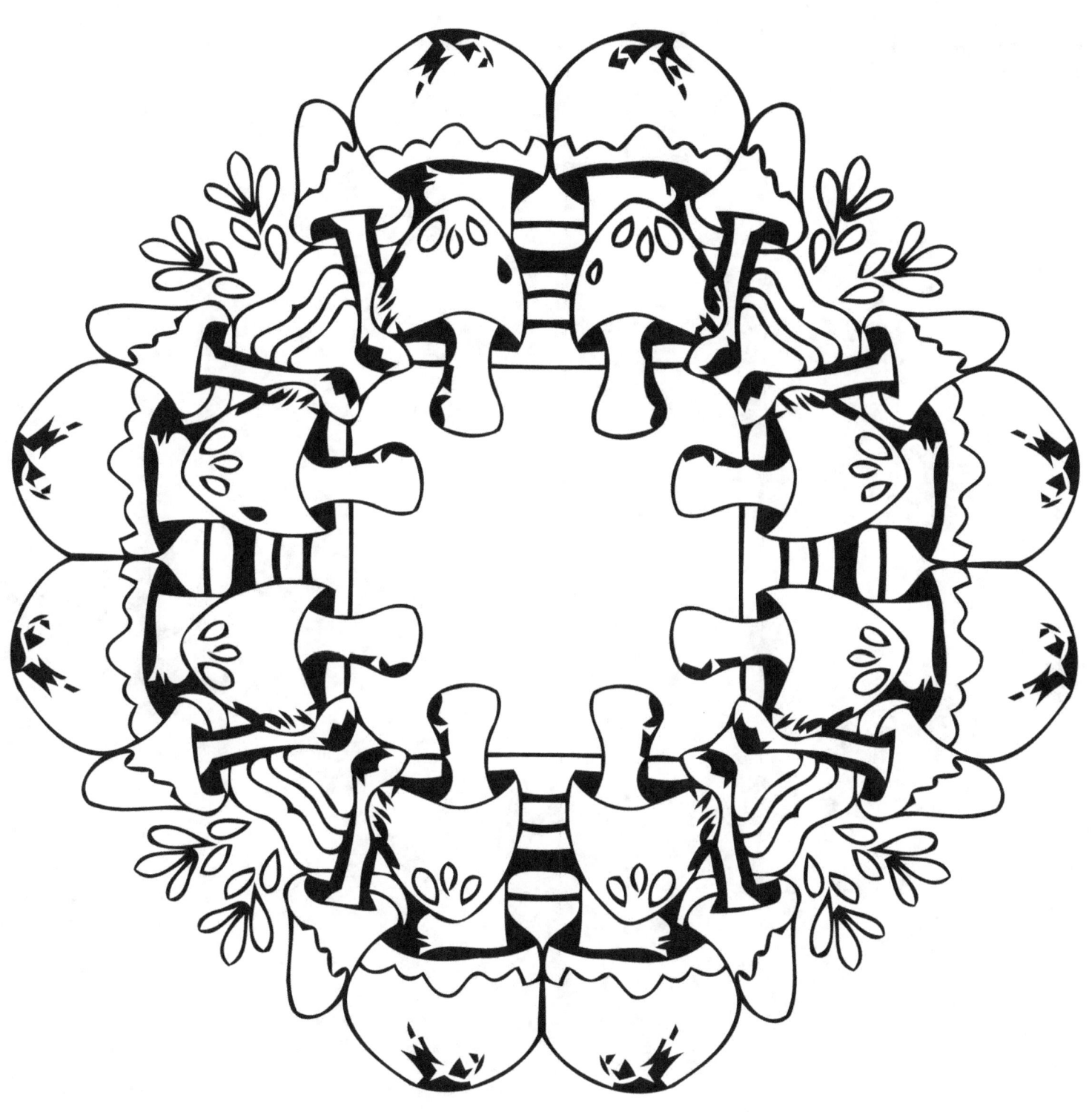

Illustrated by #cherylcolors
www.facebook.com/cherylcolors

Colored by: _____

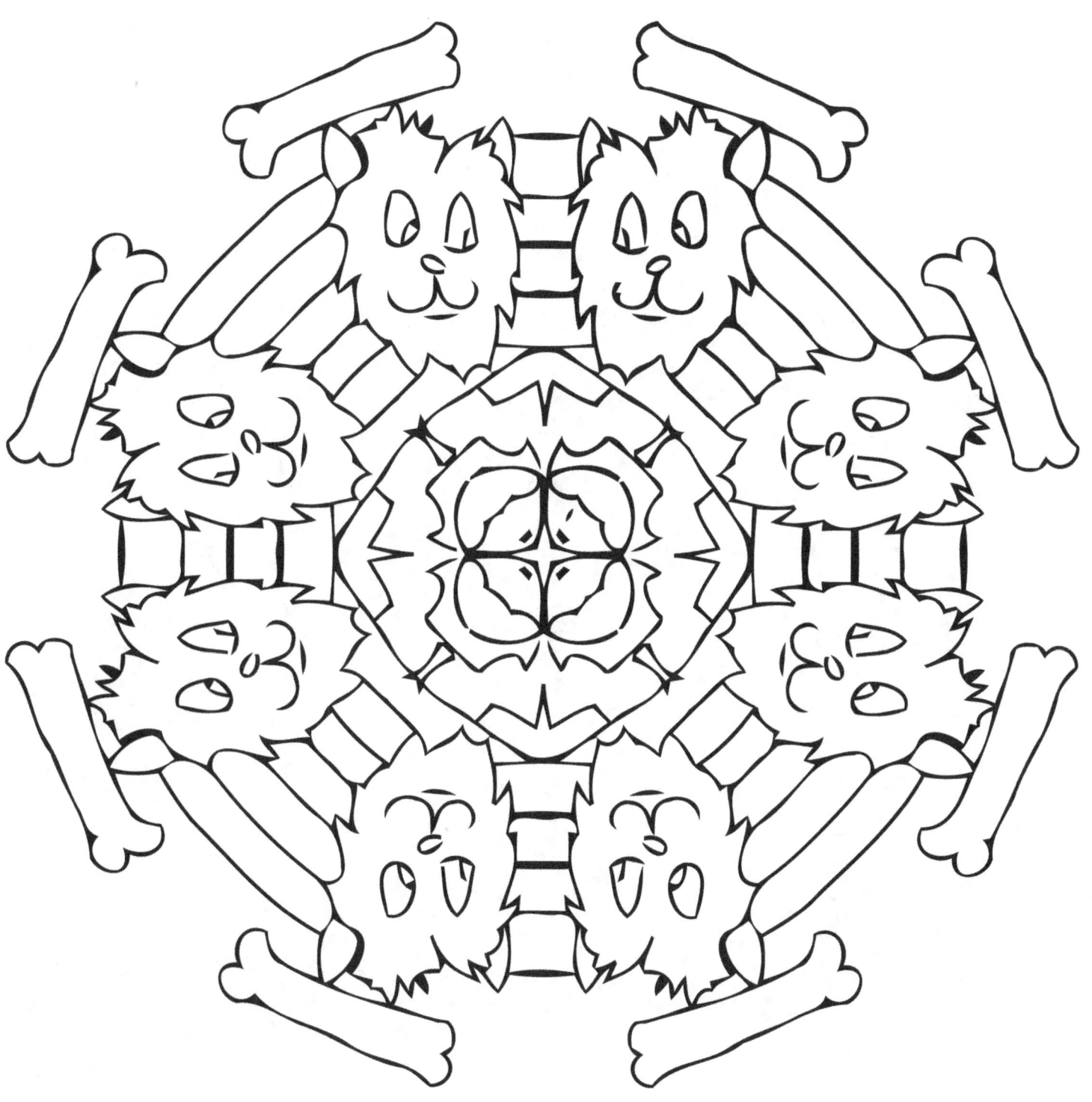

Illustrated by #cherylcolors
www.facebook.com/cherylcolors

Colored by: _____

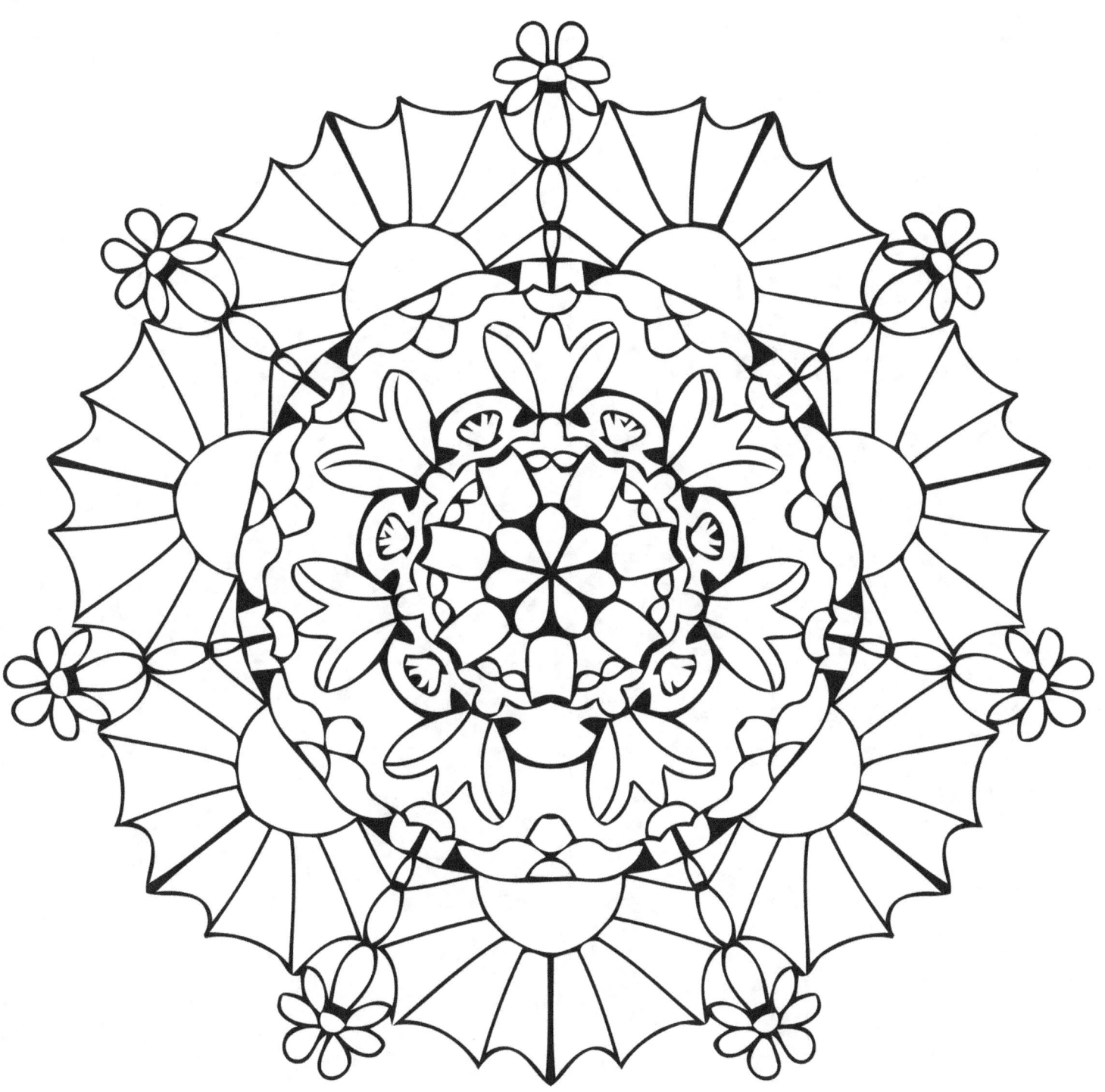

Illustrated by #cherylcolors
www.facebook.com/cherylcolors

Colored by: _____

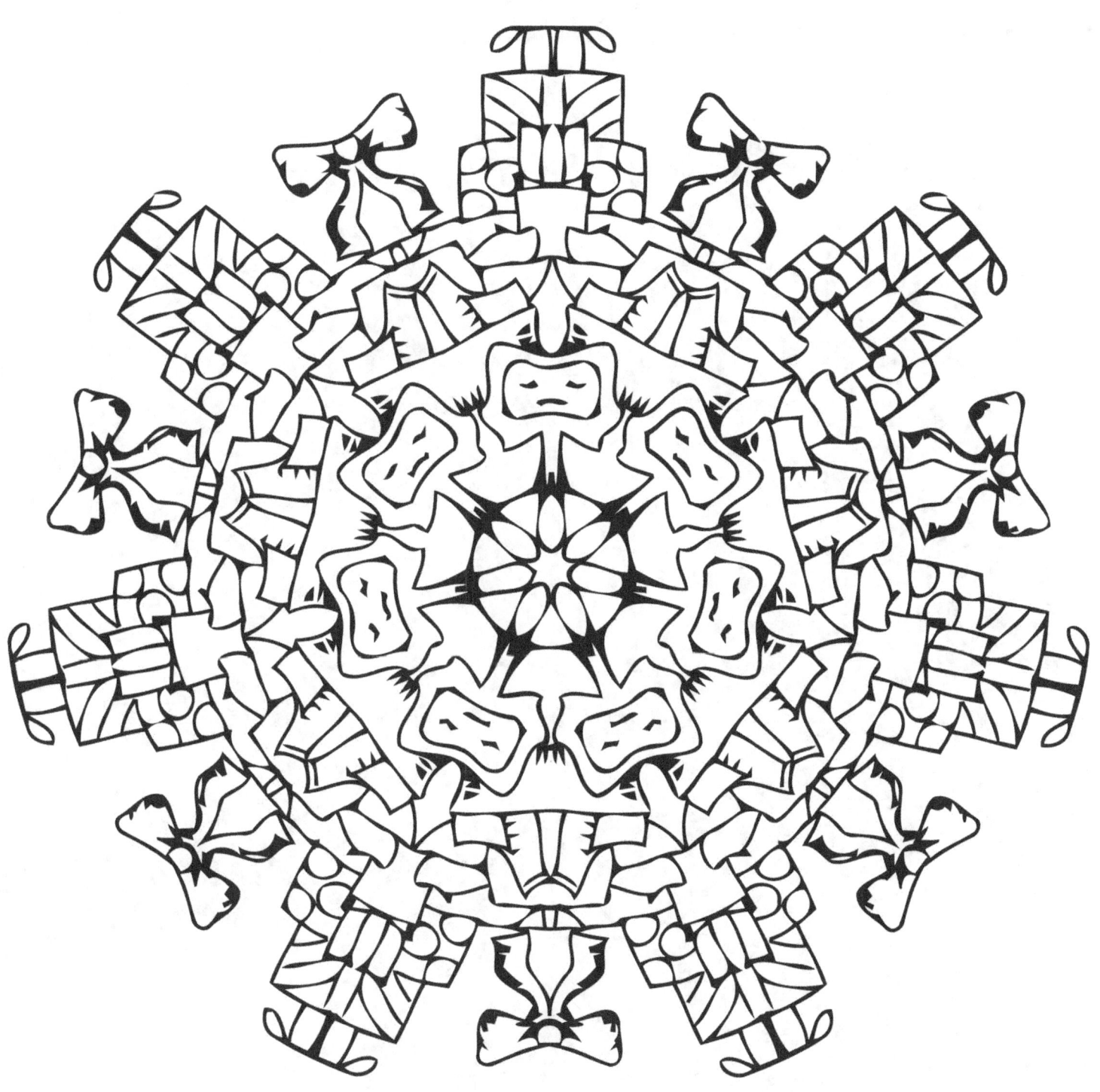

Illustrated by #cherylcolors
www.facebook.com/cherylcolors

Colored by: _____

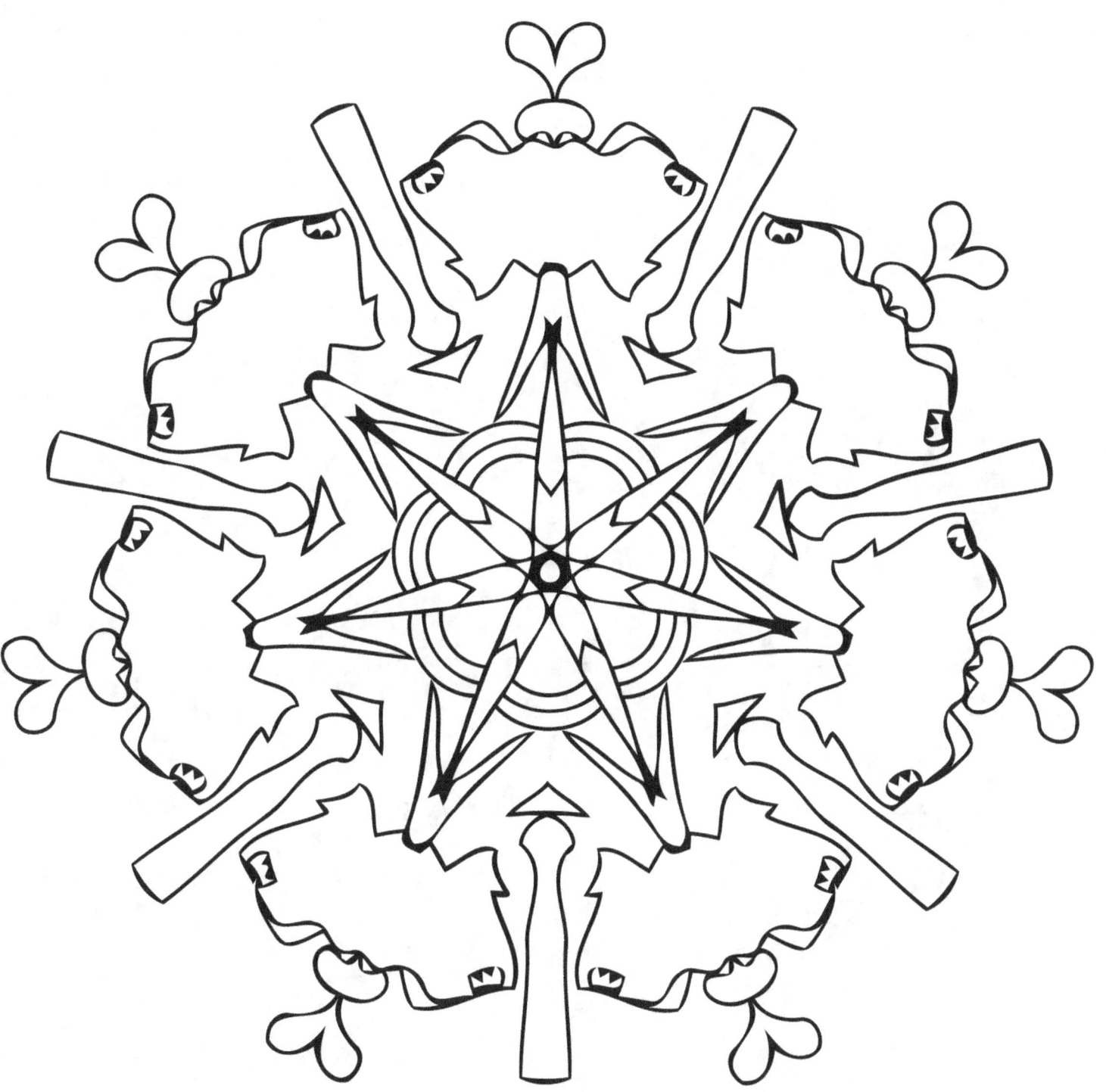

Illustrated by #cherylcolors
www.facebook.com/cherylcolors

Colored by: _____

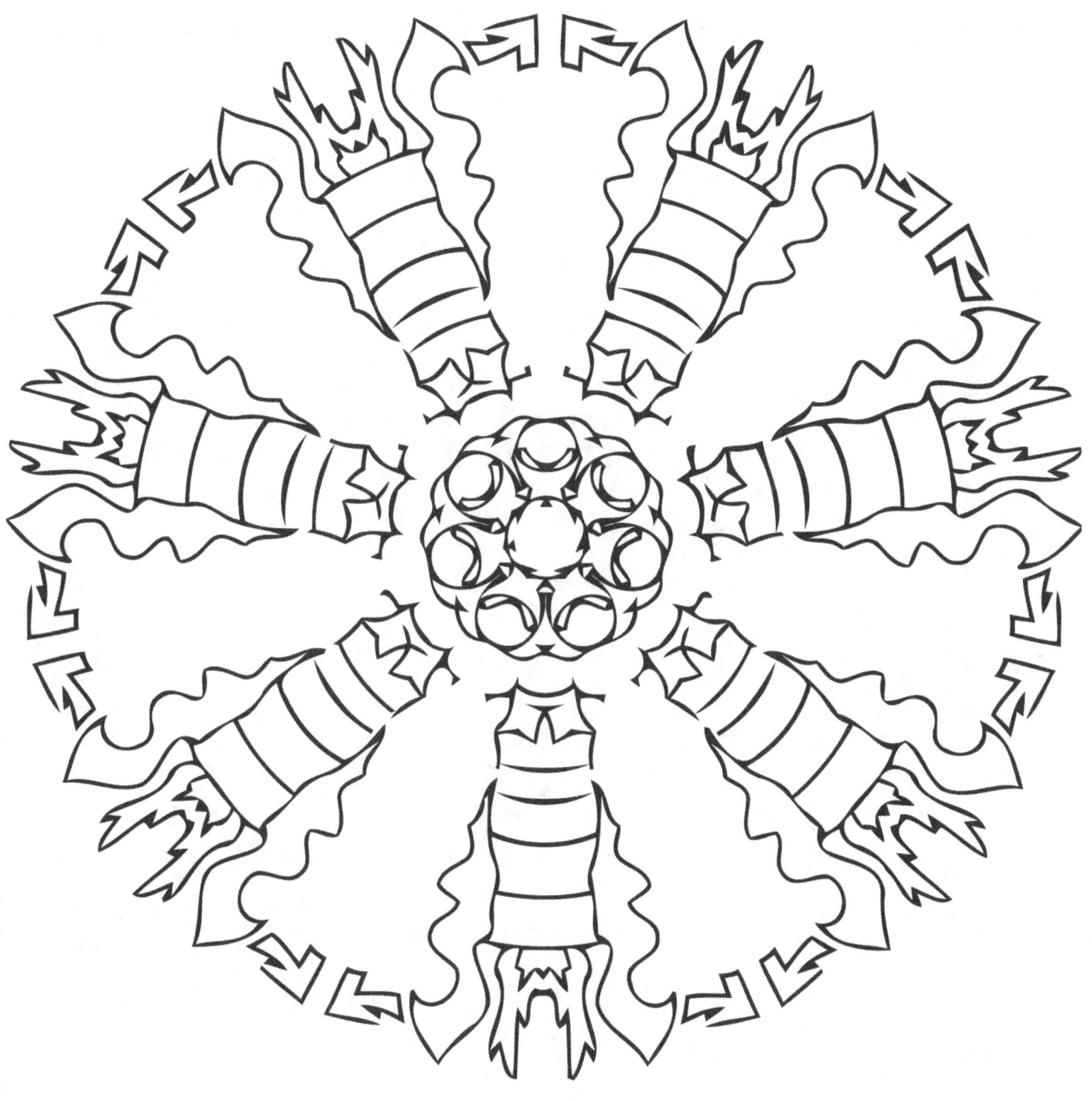

Illustrated by #cherylcolors
www.facebook.com/cherylcolors

Colored by: _____

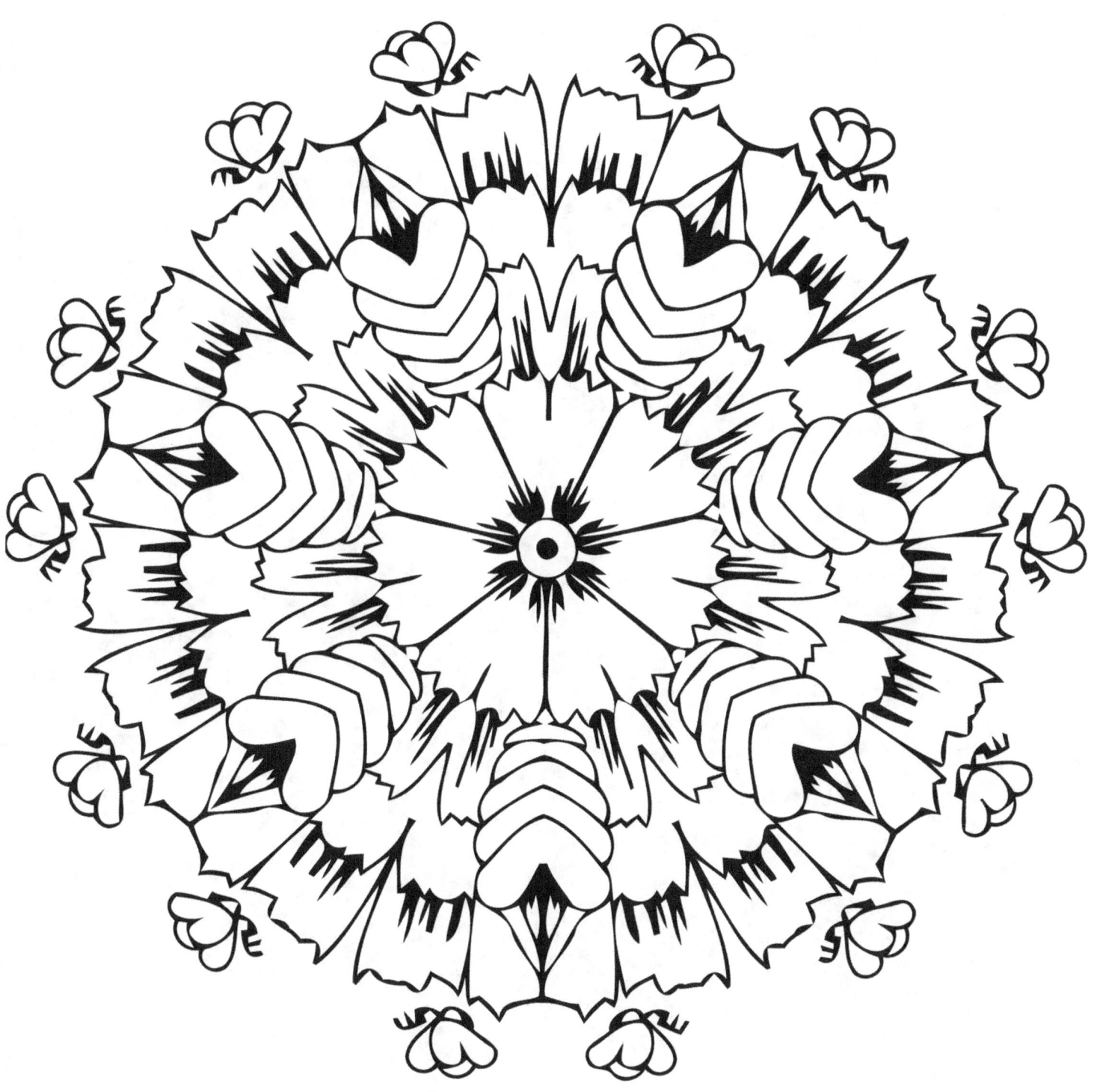

Illustrated by #cherylcolors
www.facebook.com/cherylcolors

Colored by: _____

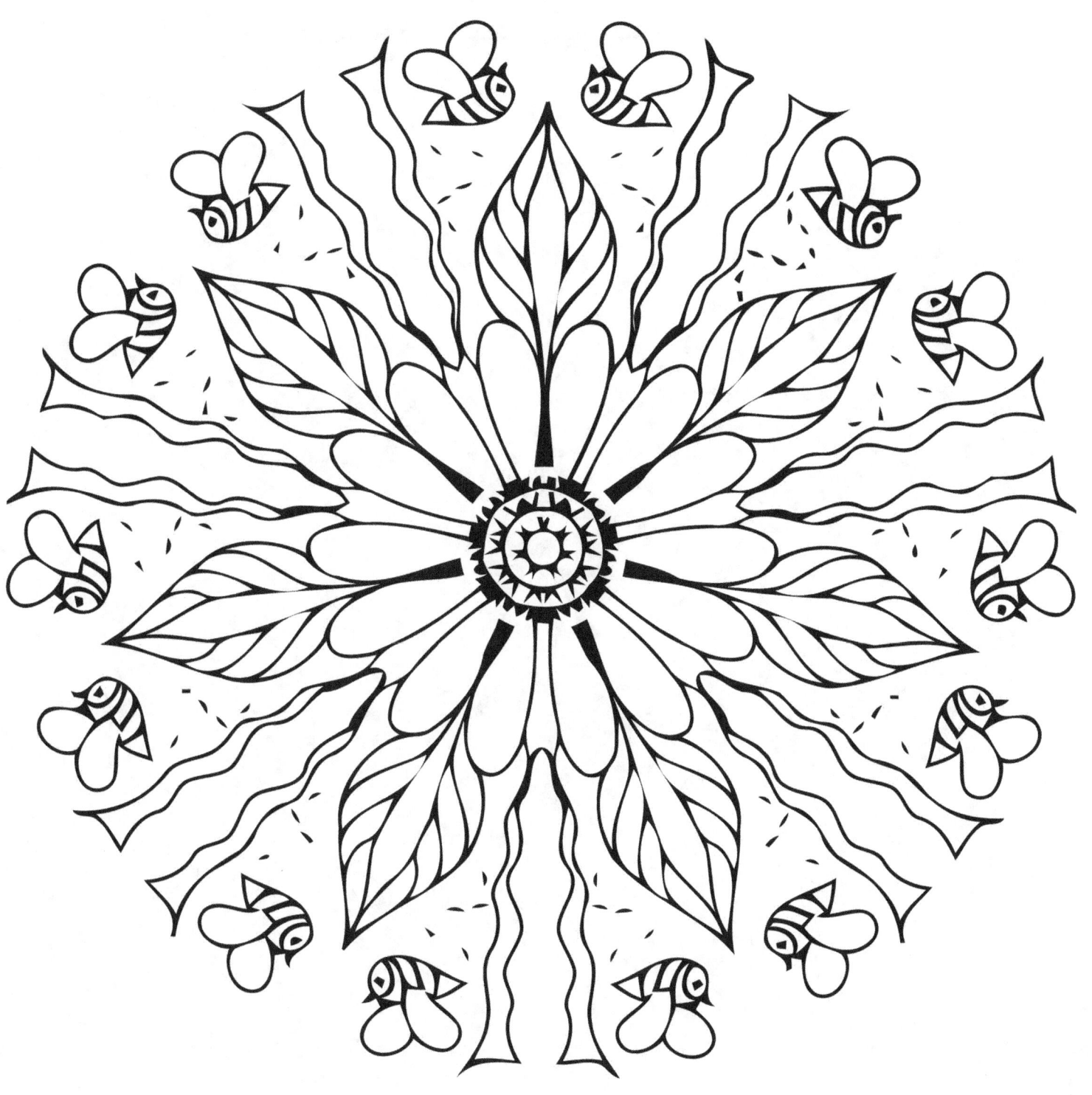

Illustrated by #cherylcolors
www.facebook.com/cherylcolors

Colored by: _____

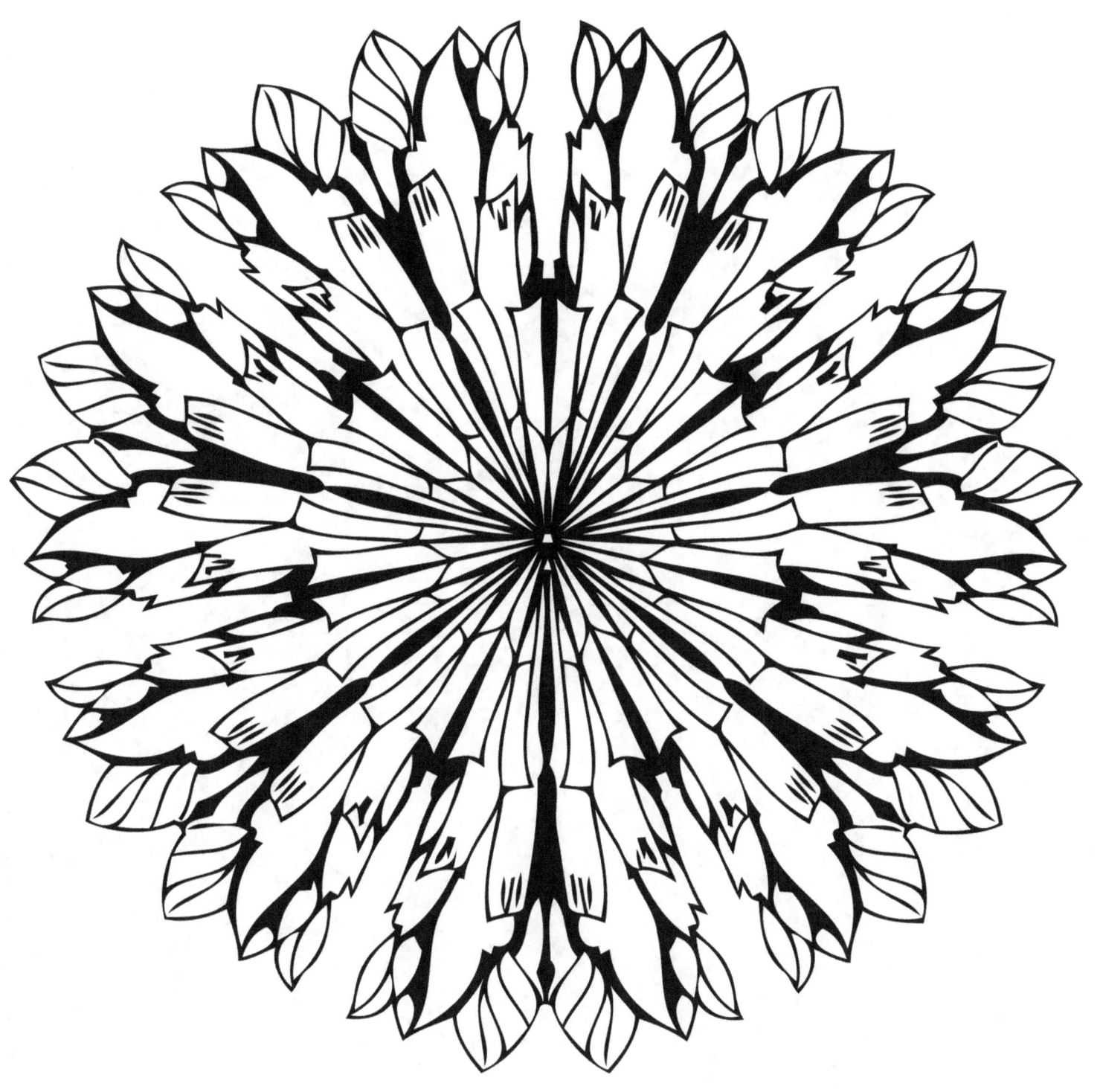

Illustrated by #cherylcolors
www.facebook.com/cherylcolors

Colored by: _____

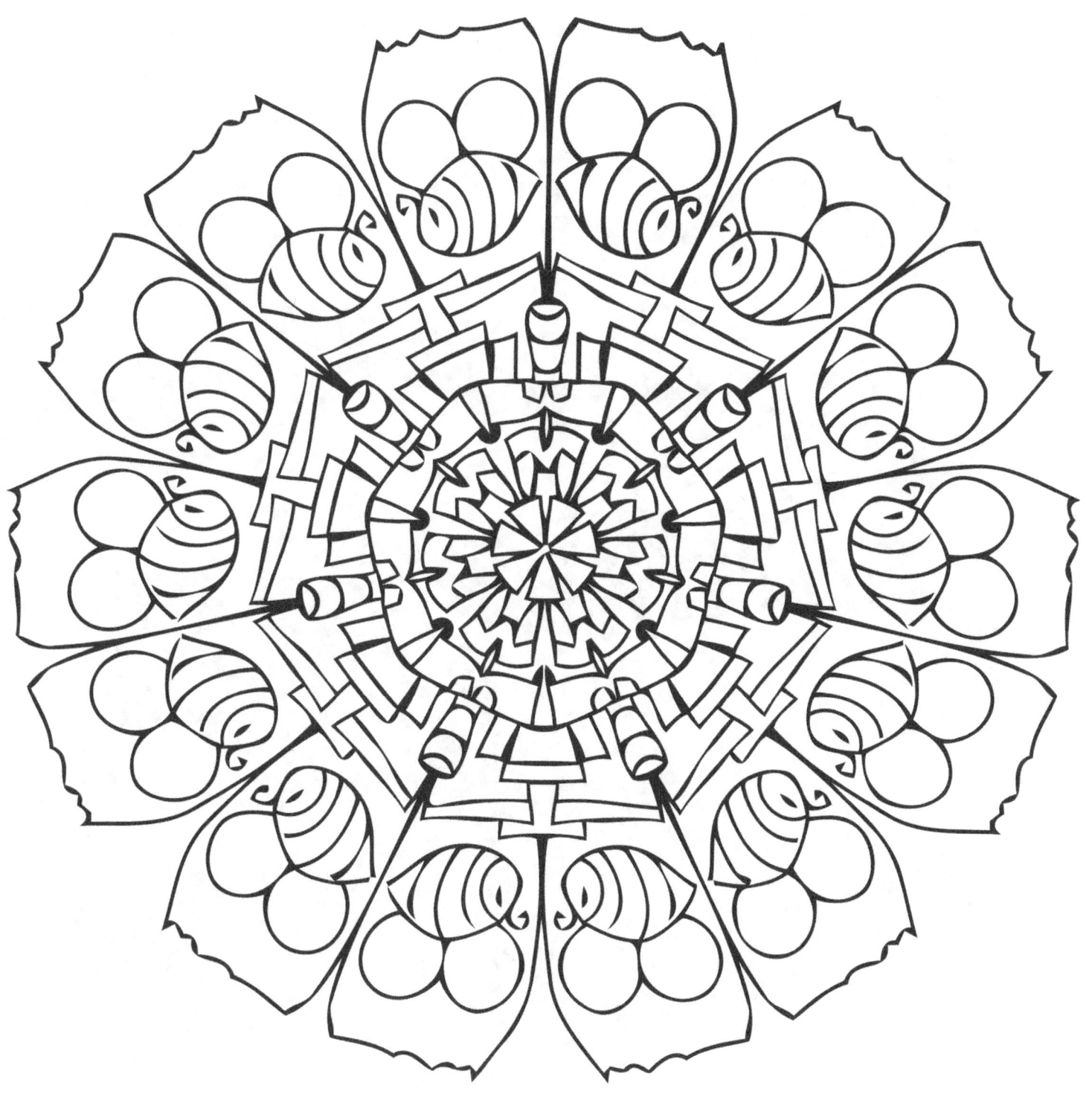

Illustrated by #cherylcolors
www.facebook.com/cherylcolors

Colored by: _____

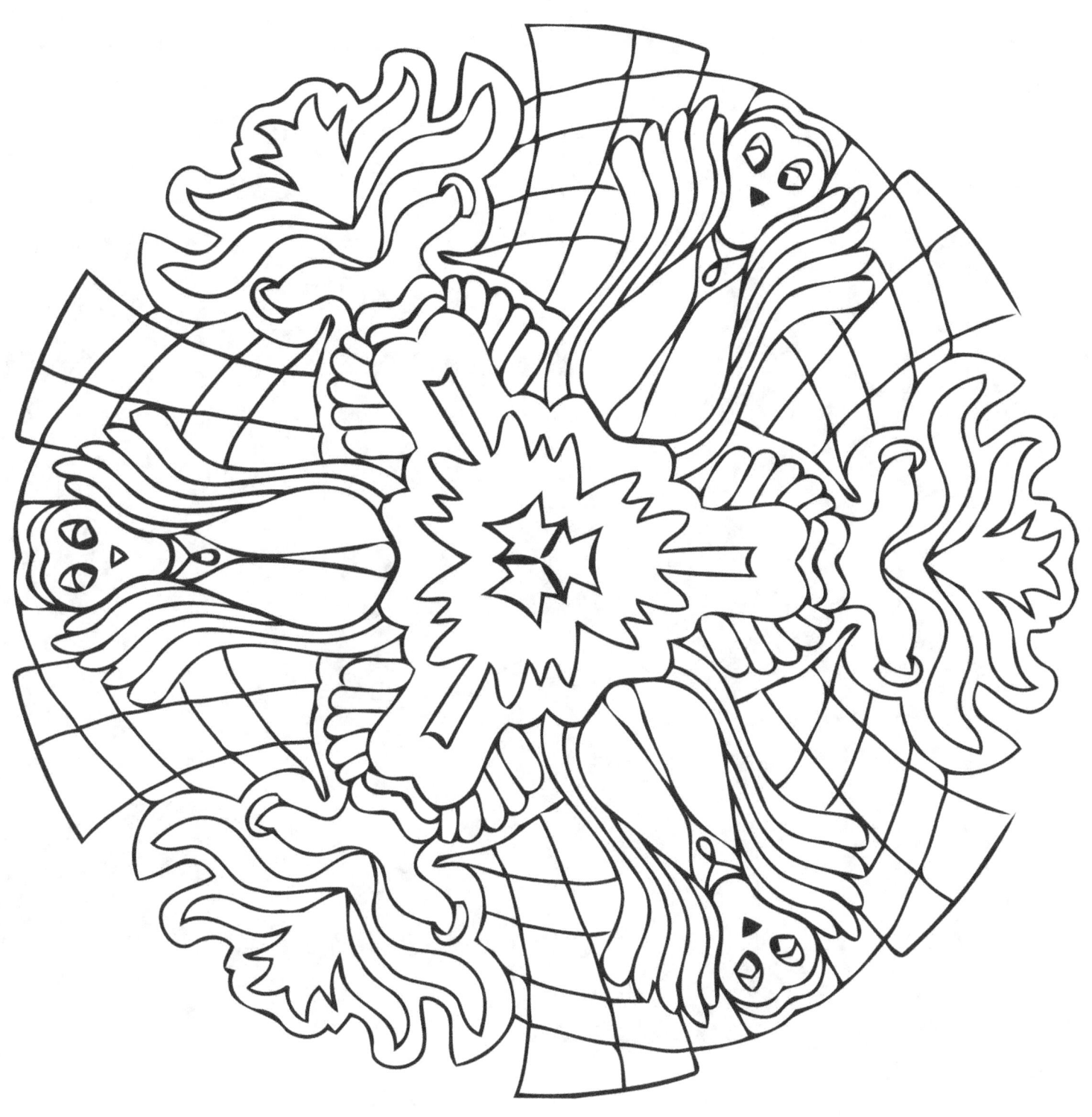

Illustrated by #cherylcolors
www.facebook.com/cherylcolors

Colored by: _____

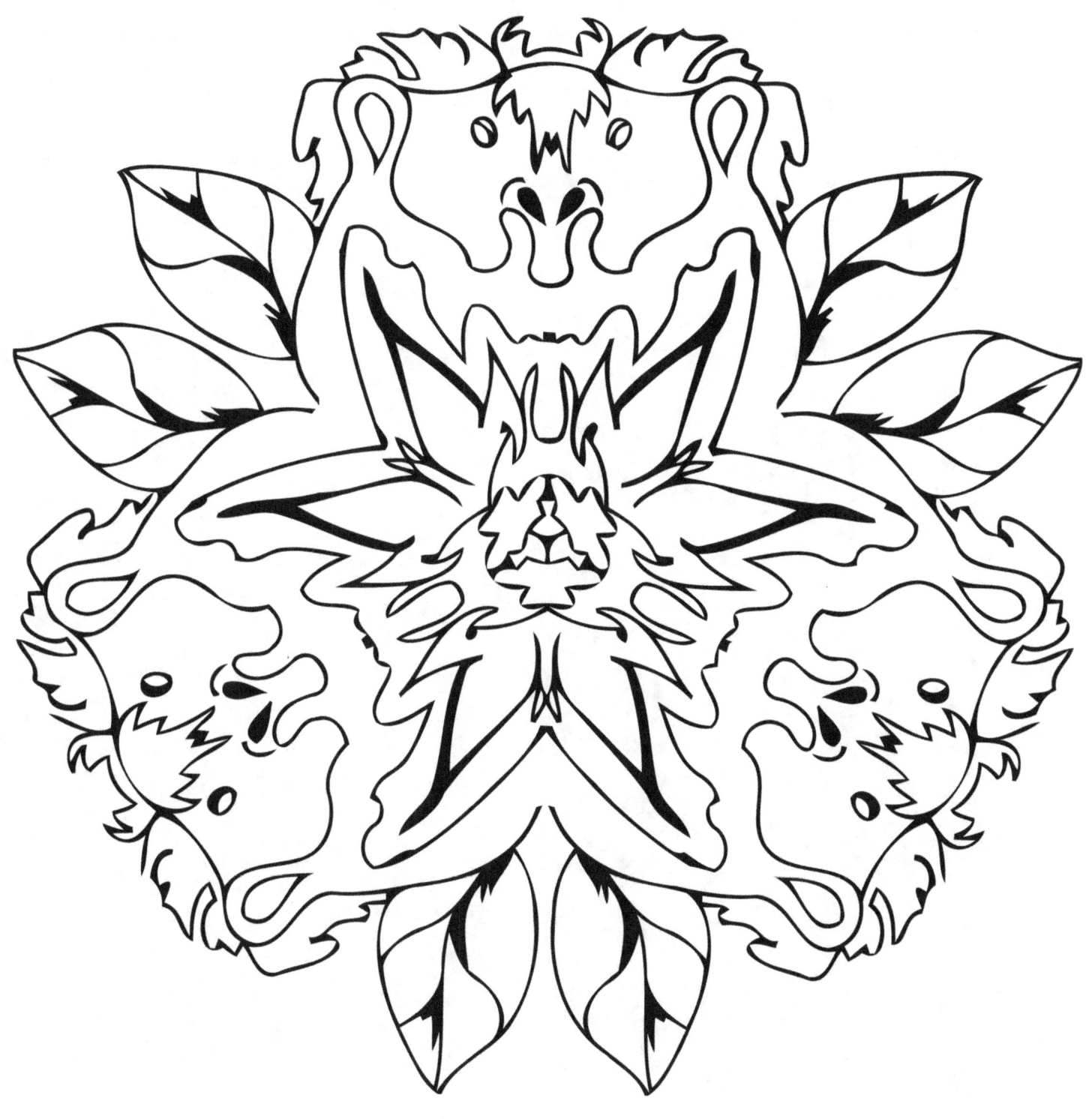

Illustrated by #cherylcolors
www.facebook.com/cherylcolors

Colored by: _____

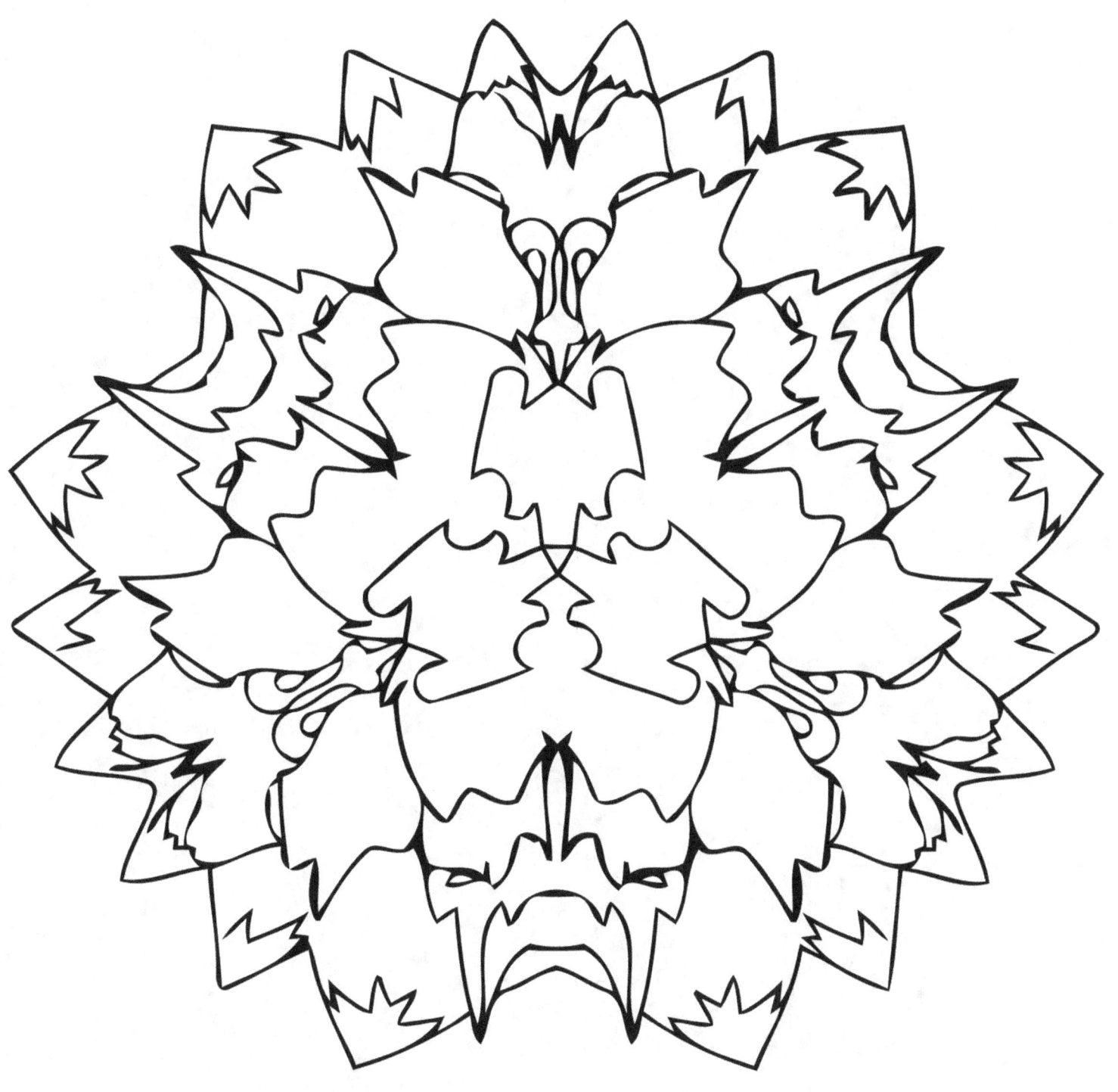

Illustrated by #cherylcolors
www.facebook.com/cherylcolors

Colored by: _____

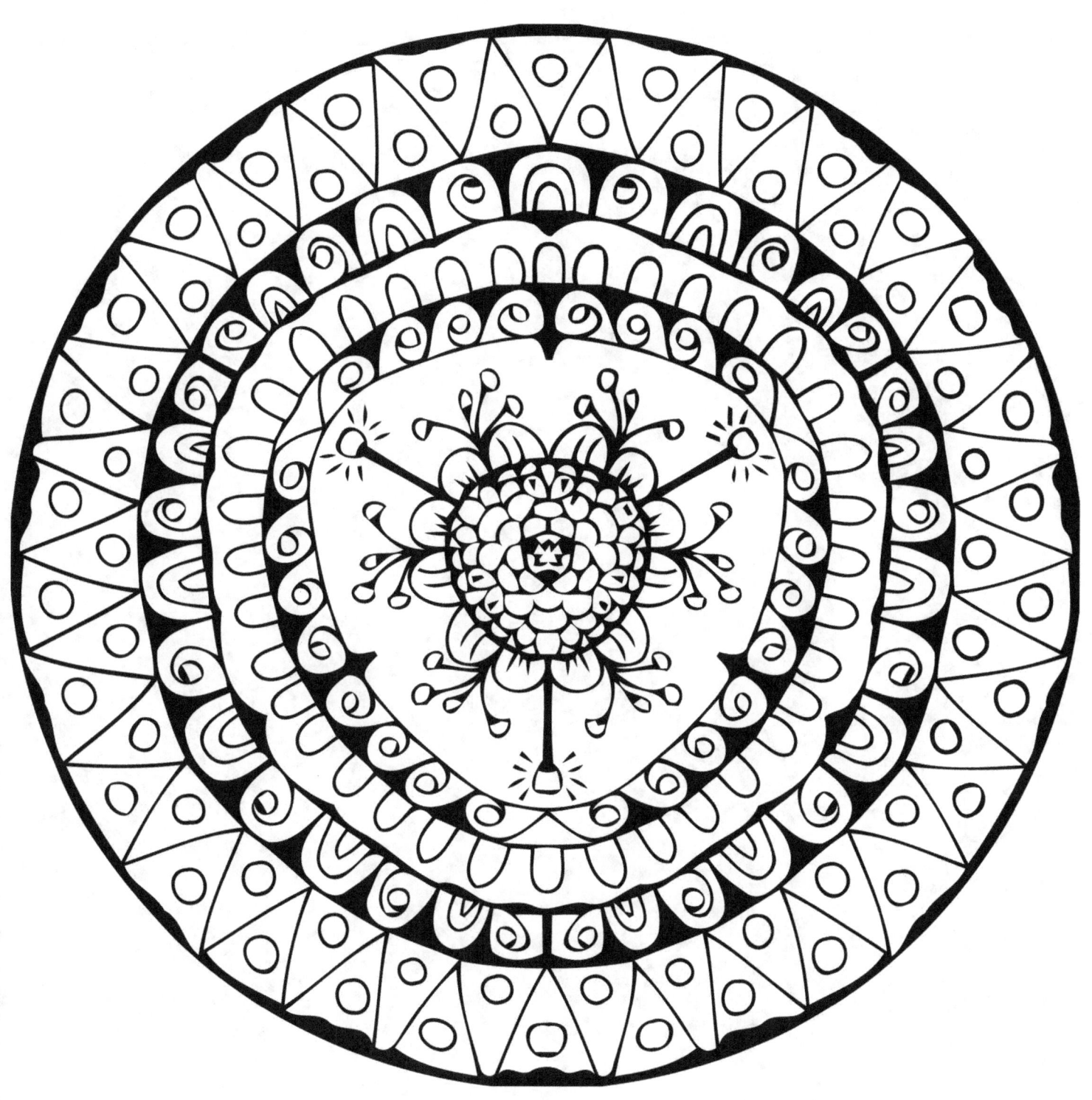

Illustrated by #cherylcolors
www.facebook.com/cherylcolors

Colored by: _____

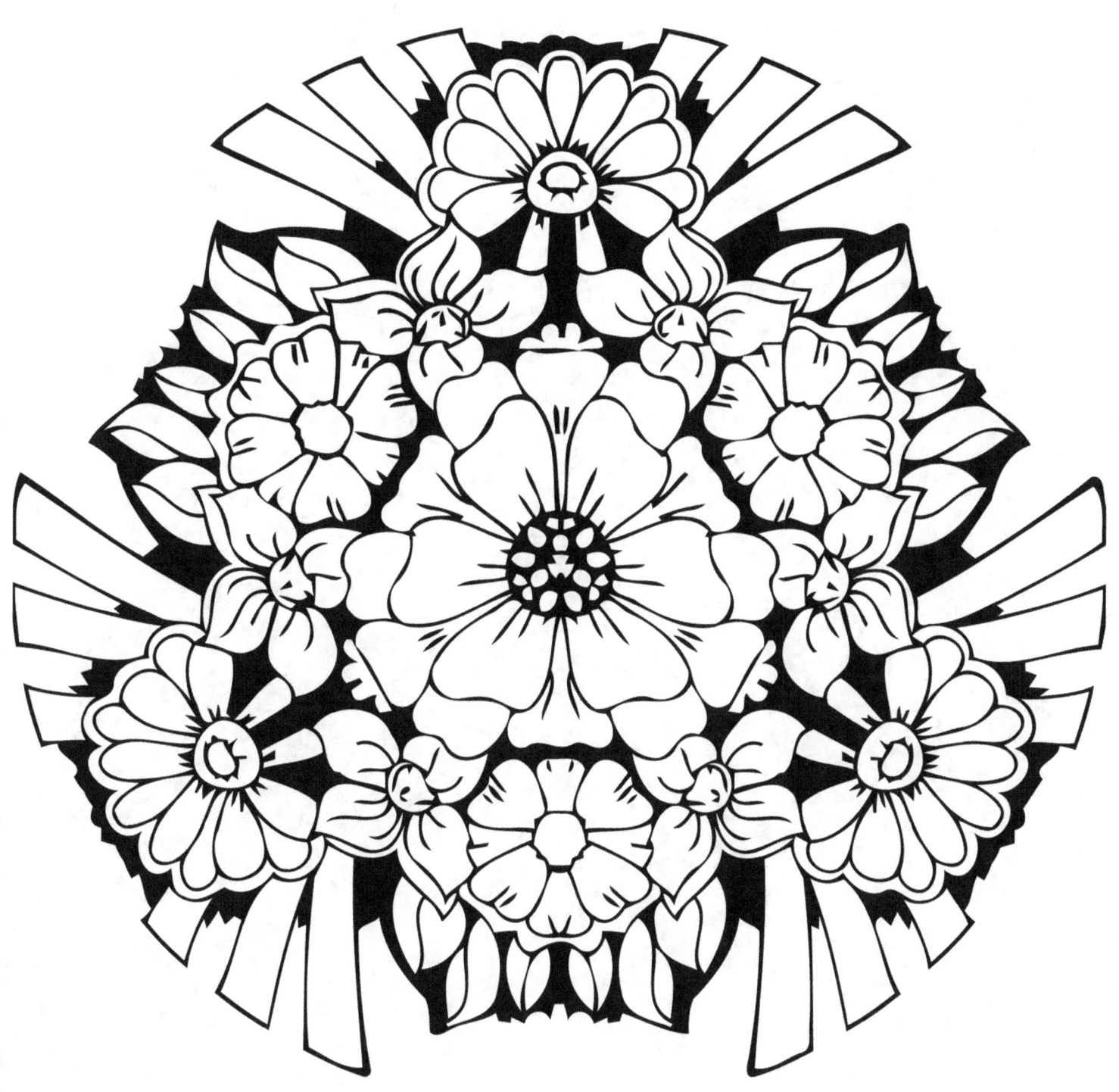

Illustrated by #cherylcolors
www.facebook.com/cherylcolors

Colored by: _____

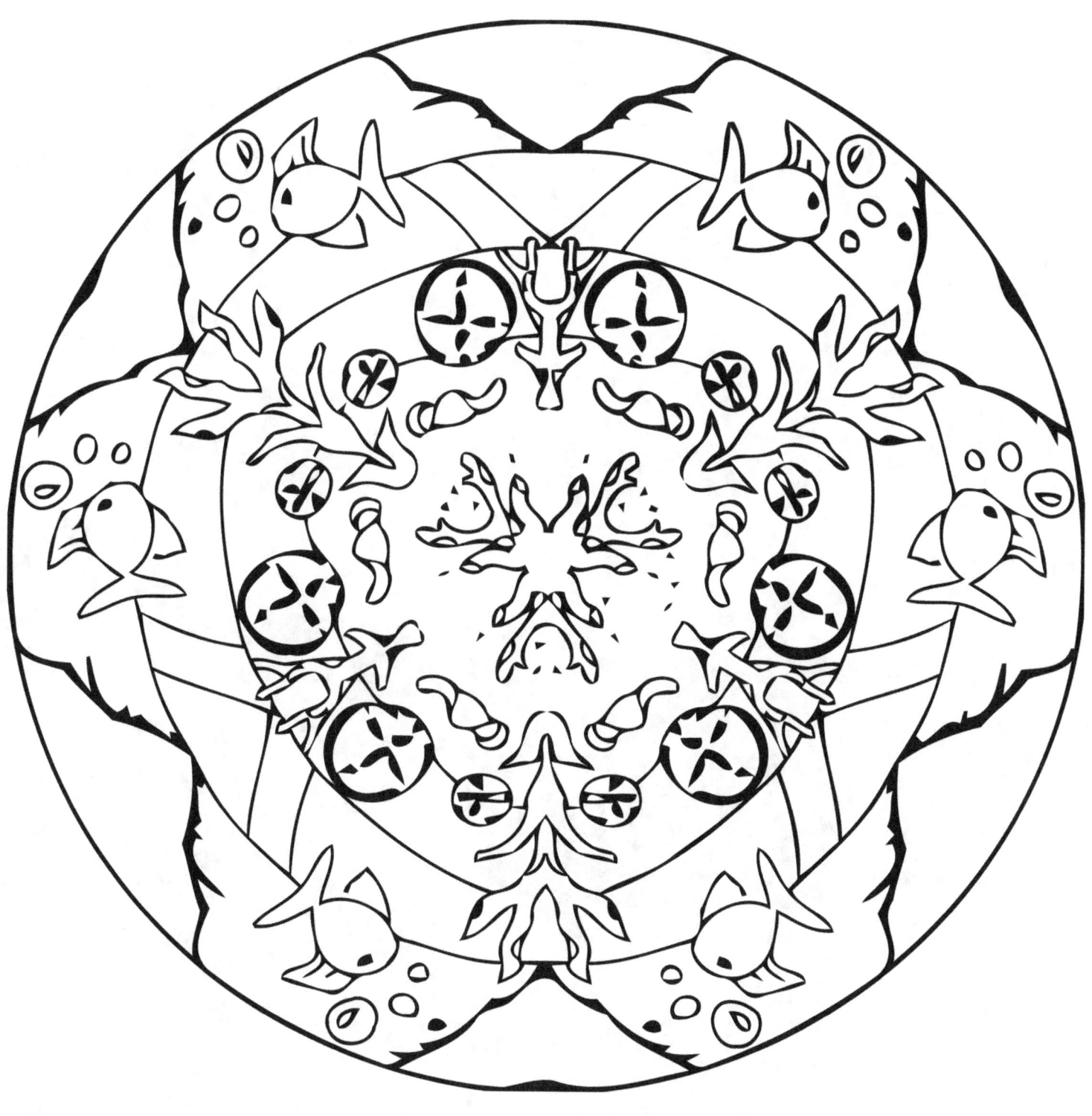

Illustrated by #cherylcolors
www.facebook.com/cherylcolors

Colored by: _____

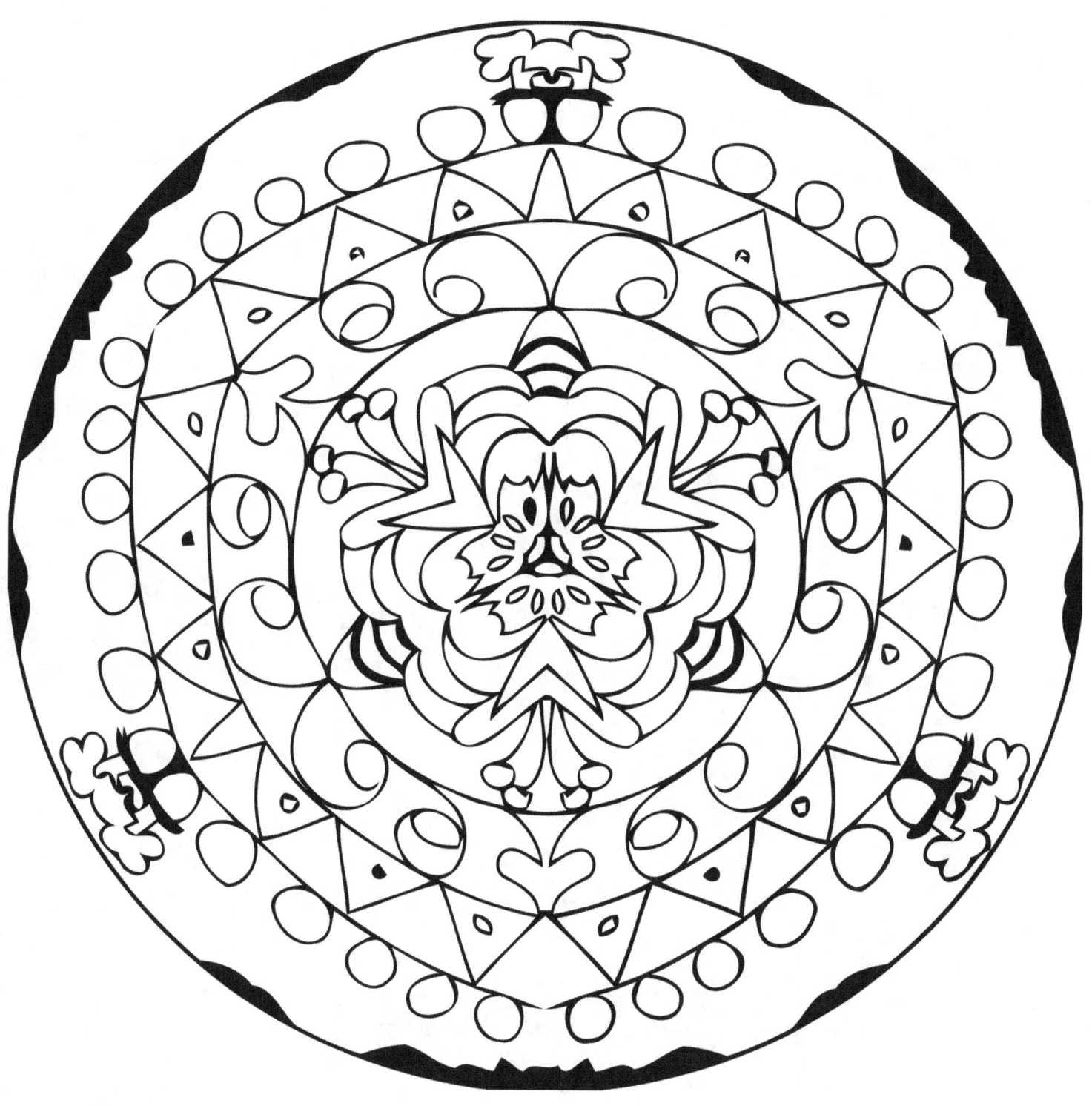

Illustrated by #cherylcolors
www.facebook.com/cherylcolors

Colored by: _____

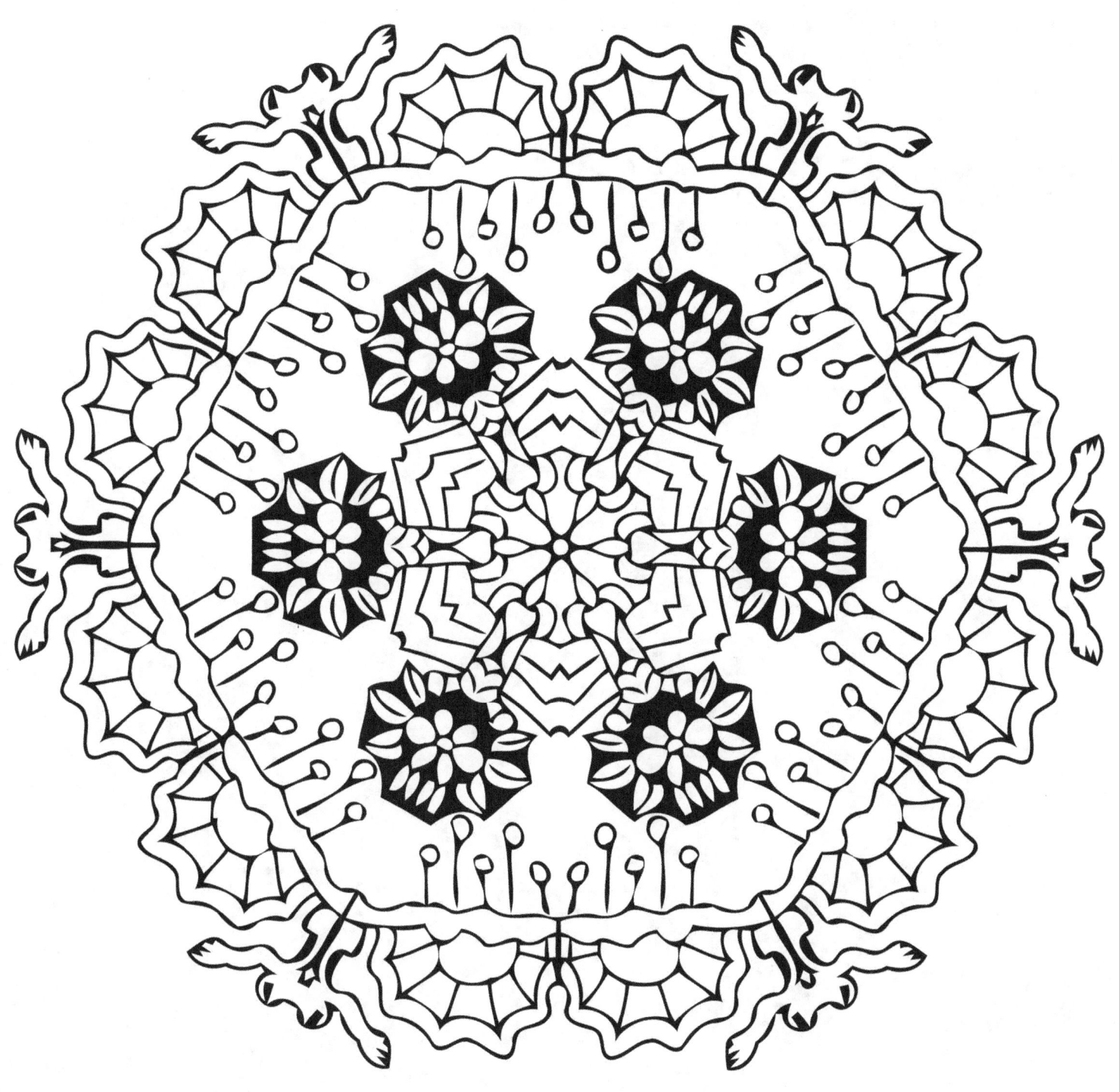

Illustrated by #cherylcolors
www.facebook.com/cherylcolors

Colored by: _____

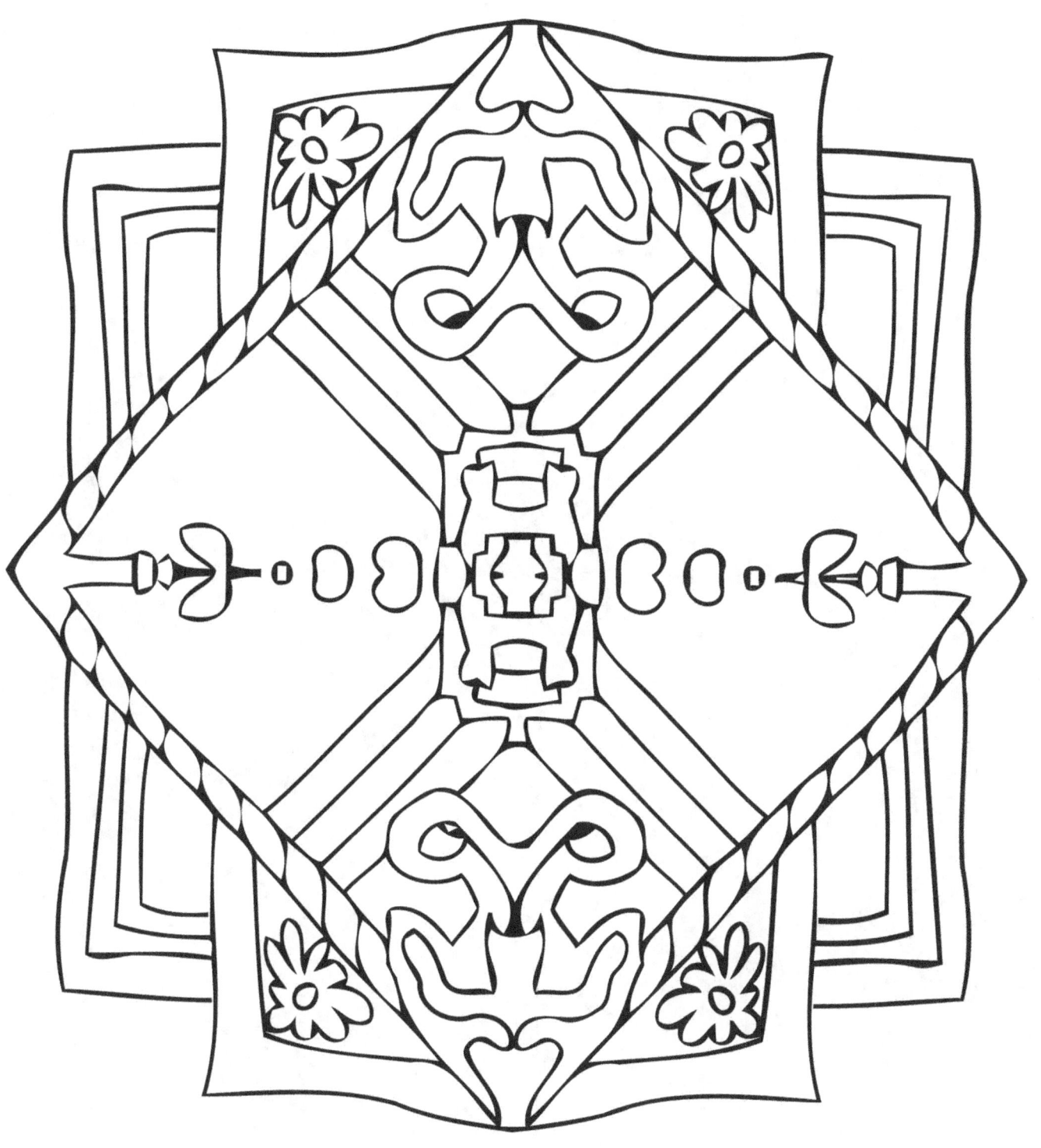

Illustrated by #cherylcolors
www.facebook.com/cherylcolors

Colored by: _____

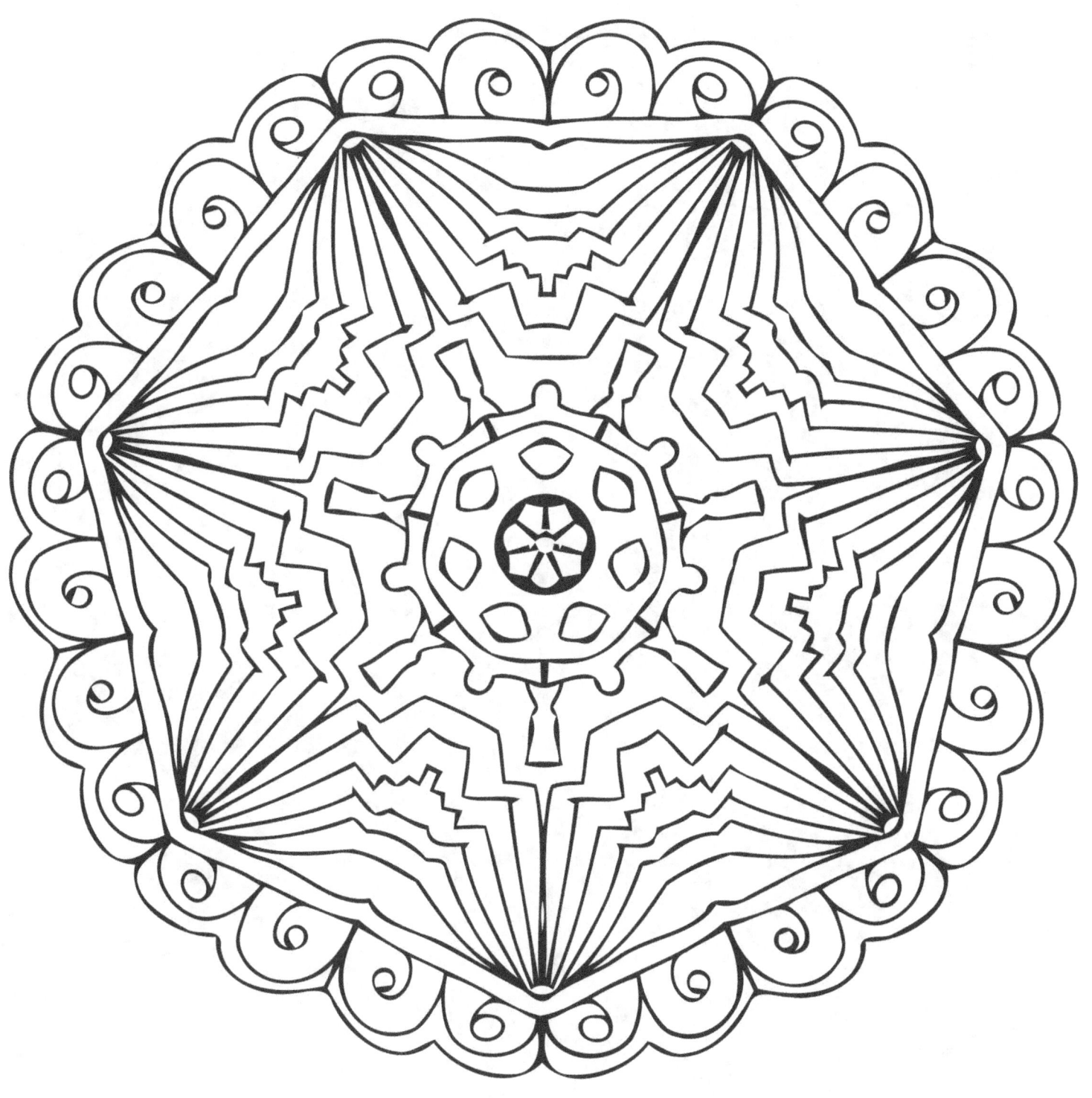

Illustrated by #cherylcolors
www.facebook.com/cherylcolors

Colored by: _____

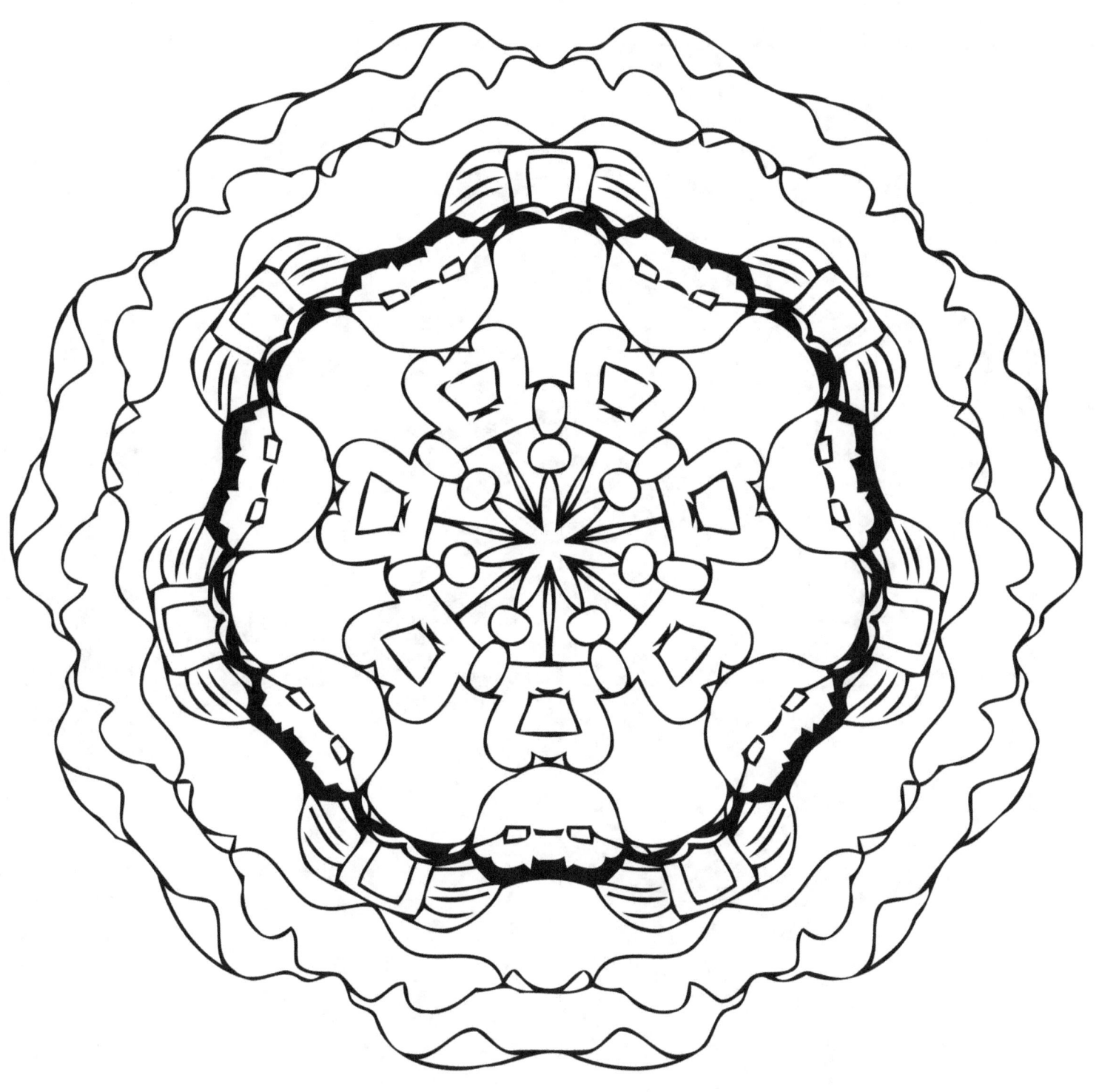

Illustrated by #cherylcolors
www.facebook.com/cherylcolors

Colored by: _____

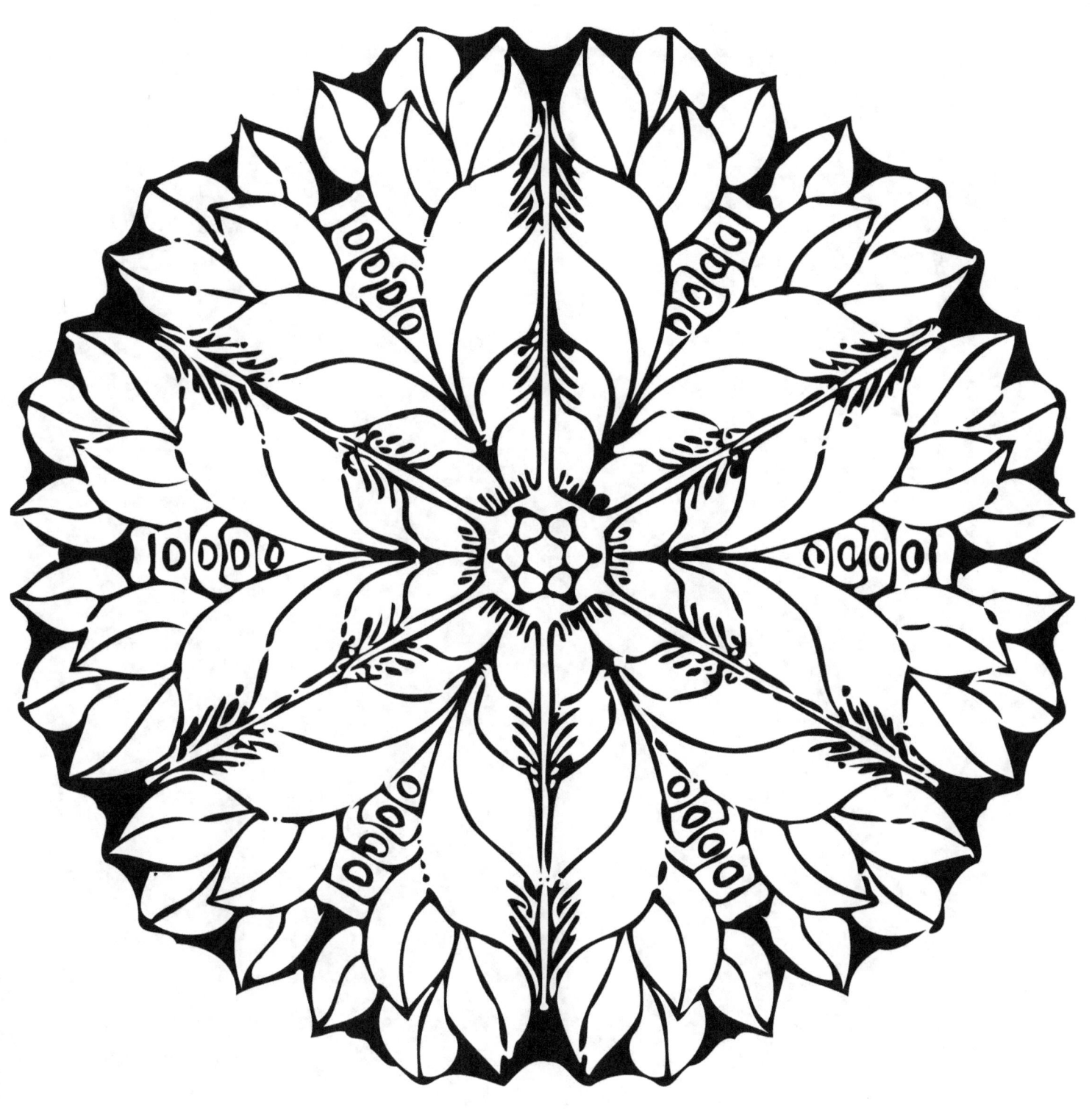

Illustrated by #cherylcolors
www.facebook.com/cherylcolors

Colored by: _____

www.ingramcontent.com/pod-product-compliance
Lightning Source LLC
Chambersburg PA
CBHW082350220526
45470CB00008B/2700